Wonderland

Beth Steel's first play *Ditch* premiered at the HighTide Festival before transferring to the Old Vic Tunnels. *Ditch* was shortlisted for the John Whiting Award. *Wonderland* is her second play and was a finalist for the Susan Smith Blackburn Prize.

BETH STEEL

Wonderland

FABER & FABER

First published in 2014
by Faber and Faber Limited
74–77 Great Russell Street, London WC1B 3DA

The right of Beth Steel to be identified as author
of this work has been asserted in accordance with
Section 77 of the Copyright, Designs and Patents Act 1988

A CIP record for this book
is available from the British Library

Typeset by Country Setting, Kingsdown, Kent CT14 8ES
Printed and bound by CPI Group (UK) Ltd, Croydon, CR0 4YY

ISBN 978–0–571–32137–7

FSC
www.fsc.org
MIX
Paper from
responsible sources
FSC® C101712

2 4 6 8 10 9 7 5 3 1

For you, Dad

Author's Note

Wonderland is a fiction based on a fact. An accurate and full account of the 1984–5 miners' strike would require a trilogy of plays; of which this is just one. Many events from that year have not been included and I have often, in the interests of drama, been inaccurate with time frames. For the best account of the miners' strike, I highly recommend Seumas Milne's *The Enemy Within*.

The play was researched and written over an isolated two-and-a-half-year period. It involved voluminous reading, going underground, listening to people's experiences above ground, and keeping faith that an ensemble play of its size from a little-known writer would find a home. That was two years ago now; since then more people have joined the play's journey, all of them I would like to thank:

My father, without whom this play would not be this play. My mother, who arranged countless phone calls at odd hours for mining tutorials, who tirelessly noted down anything I'd find useful, and whose encouragement saw me through this. Amy, my first and most imaginative reader. Dave Douglass, whose insights on the strike were invaluable and for inviting me to Barnsley. David Godber, Ian Lavery and Paul Porthouse for sharing their experiences; special thanks to Paul for coming to London and sharing his knowledge and passion for mining with the cast. UK Coal and especially Derek Main for arranging unforgettable underground visits to both Welbeck and Thoresby Collieries. Ian Hunter and Colin Murray, for taking us underground. Jennie Miller, the most tenacious and energetic agent. Ian Rickson, a stranger who I begged to read the play when no one had, who did, and whose comments helped it into the world. James Grieve and Richard Twyman: champions of the play. William Mortimer, inspired literary manager. Scott Ambler and Ashley Martin Davis for their artistry, dedication, and for coming underground. Lin and Ken Craig for their generous support and excitement. Arts Council England for a much needed grant. Paul Mason. David Hare. All the staff at the Hampstead Theatre. All the production team. Special thanks to Greg Ripley-Duggan, undaunted producer, whose belief in this play and writer has seen him do everything to ensure the best production possible.

But most of all, Edward Hall, because without him, without his ambition, courage and theatrical imagination, this play would not have had a home, and his visionary production has made it more than worth the wait.

Finally, Rowan, for everything.

I write this at the end of the second week of rehearsal and already it is clear that the staging of the play will (and I believe always should) differ from what is described here. But I have decided to keep the original stage directions that includes the use of 'above' and 'below' rather than convey the more integrated staging by which it will be done, nor have I described the detailed work logic in the mine that underpins the staging for many of the early scenes. These imaginings, and more besides, are Edward Hall's and it does not feel right to appropriate them as my own. The text itself, however, will barely differ from the play as performed.

Wonderland was first performed at Hampstead Theatre, London, on 20 June 2014. The cast, in alphabetical order, was as follows:

Bobbo Nigel Betts
Colonel Paul Brennen
David Hart Dugald Bruce-Lockhart
Spud Gunnar Cauthery
Nicholas Ridley Paul Cawley
Ian Macgregor Michael Cochrane
Jimmy Ben-Ryan Davies
Peter Walker Andrew Havill
Malcom David Moorst
Fanny Paul Rattray
Milton Friedman / Chief of Police Andrew Readman
Tilsley Simon Slater

Additional parts played by members of the cast

Director Edward Hall
Assistant Director Tom Attenborough
Designer Ashley Martin Davis
Lighting Peter Mumford
Choreographer Scott Ambler
Sound Matt McKenzie
Composer Simon Slater

Characters

Tilsley
manager

Colonel
pitman

Bobbo
pitman

Fanny
pitman

Spud
pitman

Jimmy
apprentice

Malcom
apprentice

Peter Walker
Energy Secretary and a wet

Nicholas Ridley
Transport Secretary and a dry

Ian MacGregor
Chairman of the National Coal Board

David Hart
officially a reporter for *The Times*

Milton Friedman

Mr Bishop

Chief
of the Metropolitan Police

Special Branch

Operative

Head Set

Daniel Hargreaves
security guard

The Time

1983–1985

The Place

London and the Midlands

WONDERLAND

Others have laboured, and ye are
entered into their labours . . .

John 4:38

Prologue

A sharp light illuminates a very small man with large spectacles and a bow tie.

Milton (*to us*) Hello. I'm Milton Friedman. And I'm an economist. It has been said that there is nothing so powerful as an idea when its time has come. I say that time is a crisis, actual *or* perceived. When the crisis occurs the actions that are taken depends upon the ideas lying around. In the economic crisis of the late 1970s, when that long period of Western prosperity died and all attempts at reviving it came to nothing, the ideas lying around were mine. Ideas so radical they tore up the economic rulebook of forty years, paving the way for a truly free market. (*Beat.*) This then is the story of that idea. The story of a country in crisis. Britain, 1983.

Act One

APPRENTICES

Welbeck Colliery, lamp room.
    The lamp room is on the pit top, a cramped space with rows of head lamps and a cage at the back. The men are jostling for their lamps. The cage is opened, they pile in, and two lads, sixteen and shitting themselves, remain and watch it plunge.

Malcom Hey-up.

Jimmy Hey-up.

    Pause.

Malcom You been down before?

    Jimmy shakes his head.

I've been down before.

Jimmy How was it?

Malcom I don't remember. It was a school trip.

Jimmy And you can't remember owt?

Malcom I passed out.

Jimmy What you doing at pit then?

Malcom (*shrugs*) It's a job, int it? (*Pause.*) You reckon we'll be going down today?

Jimmy I reckon so.

Malcom I thought they'd show us around first.

Jimmy What's to see – except for what's down there?

Malcom We've got all pit top to look at.

Jimmy That's true.

Malcom They'll start us off with a tour, won't they?

Jimmy We need to know our way around I suppose.

Malcom That's what I'm thinking.

They settle into a quiet reassurance, until . . .

Jimmy Why were we told to wait here then, in lamp room?

Malcom Could just be a meeting point?

Jimmy Why were we given these hats if we're *not* going underground?

Malcom You can't walk around pit top without a hat.

Jimmy That's true. We'll no doubt have to run through some procedures as well.

Malcom After the tour?

Jimmy If we've got time, yeah.

Malcom If not we can always do that tomorrow.

Colonel (*offstage*) Right then, you little shits, *get your knickers on*!

Jimmy and Malcom look at each other and sling their hard hats on.
   Enter the Colonel. He looks at the lads before him.

(*Depressed sigh.*) We'll start with the paperwork.

He lifts his hard hat, produces a scrap of paper, and a small pen from his ear.

Name?

Malcom Malcom.

Colonel And the rest, youth.

Malcom Malcom Mervin Blenkinsop.

Colonel Any chance you're related to Frank Herbert Blenkinsop?

Malcom He's my brother.

Colonel I gave him his induction when he started – how's he getting on?

Malcom He's left the pit.

Colonel Thank fuck for that. What is that bright star doing?

Malcom Nowt. He got a job over at tinning factory then they all got made redundant.

Colonel And don't tell me, now he's thinking of coming back to pit.

Malcom Aye, if he can.

Colonel Then I shall personally see to it that he fucking can't. Name?

Jimmy Jimmy Warren.

Malcom Are we going underground today?

Colonel How old are you?

Malcom Sixteen.

Colonel You?

Jimmy Same.

Colonel You shoulda been down there two year ago! Where the fuck have you lads been?

Jimmy We've been at school, haven't we?

Colonel What for – did you pass owt?

Jimmy No.

Malcom I did. I got two!

Colonel What you need to be a miner is a healthy attitude to work, which you must already be in possession of, 'cause if you dint like back-breaking graft you wouldn't have to come to pit. The other thing is common sense. Which you will *not* be in possession of. But will learn from me during your apprenticeship. That is of course unless you quit. There's always them that quits. Why is that, youth?

Malcom Er . . . they don't like it?

Colonel They can't *hack* it. That's why. Your brother dint tell you that, did he? No doubt he told you that he dint want to be miner after all. That he'd rather be an electrician, a mechanic, come to think of it . . . a *rock star*. That he's his own man. That at the grand old age of seventeen he don't need to stand there taking bollockings from a handsome fucker like me. Do you thrive on a good bollocking?

Malcom I think so.

Colonel Then we shall get along.

Colonel pulls two lamps off the rack and hands them to the lads.

Every miner's got his own lamp with his check number stamped on it *and* on the rack where he keeps it. If there's an incident, a gas leak, we'll know you're still underground if your lamp's not on rack.

Colonel produces small tokens, motties, and hands them out.

These are your motties. One goes to pay office and you keep other one with you at all times. If there's a disaster, an explosion, then rescue team use it to identify you.

7

Colonel points to a small metal box attached to the belts around their waists.

This is your self-rescuer for an underground fire. It's got a mask inside it with twenty minutes' worth of oxygen and it's a complete waste of time. Same as being on a plane, if you have to wear one of these you know you're fucked. Where we're working is three miles in, if there is a fire we're dead. Any questions? That's that then.

He makes towards the cage.

Malcom That's it?

Colonel Got a question there, youth?

Malcom That's all the procedures?

Colonel Aye.

They stare at the open cage. Then pile on in and make their descent . . .
Pit bottom: jet black, ghostly atmosphere, a rattling wind.
Out of the cage they step, head lamps blinking on, they stand in silence.

Jimmy Where's all coal?

Colonel Did they not tell you you had to work for it?

Malcom I still can't see owt.

Colonel You've not got your lamp on. There's only coal on face.

Jimmy It's like another world.

Colonel It is. It's our world.

They walk down the shaft until they arrive at two carts, like sledges but with wheels, a stretch of rope attached to each and set on top of what looks like train tracks.

Colonel This is the haulage. Materials are loaded on to your cart at the beginning of the shift. You then pull the cart to the coaling face, that's just shy of a mile, and unload it. Then you load the empty cart with any scrap from the coaling face and bring it back here. You'll not be doing more than one trip a shift. First, there's about three times your body weight in there. Second, the further you get into the pit the hotter she gets. Any questions? That's that then. (*Smiles.*) Your job for next six months.

The lads look at each other and at the stretch of tracks before them.

HARD GRAFT

Underground: off the coaling face.
Fanny and Spud appear. They wear Y-fronts, pit boots and hats only; lathered in sweat, they are like run-out racehorses. Spud is a wiry slip of a thing. Fanny is built like a loaf of soggy bread.

Spud Christ. I'm thirsty.

Fanny I've got a tongue as dry as Gandhi's flip-flop.

Spud Give us your flask then.

He looks at Fanny, sees he has no flask.

Fanny I thought you'd brought yours.

Spud Do I look like I'm carrying a flask?

Fanny I left mine in lamp room.

Spud What's it doing there?

Fanny (*shrugs sheepishly*) Lorraine said I'd lose my balls if they weren't in a bag.

Spud Alright, let's have a minute.

They sit, stretch out their legs; take snuff.

I wonder what weather's doing.

Fanny Supposed to be sunny.

Spud I hope we get some.

Fanny We going for a pint?

Spud I'm meeting Christina.

Fanny She still married?

Spud Her husband's away on 'business'.

Fanny Guess so then.

Spud I'm going over to their house.

Fanny You're not gonna give her one there, are you?

Spud Course not, I'm giving her three at least. Bounce her until her eyes cross.

Fanny I don't agree with that: taking the jam out of another man's sandwich.

Spud I'll tell you something else, she's got a *waterbed*.

Fanny A waterbed?

Spud She told me *all* about it on phone.

Fanny I don't think I'd fancy that.

Spud Open your mind to the possibilities. I'm gonna get her doing some breast stroke.

Fanny I think I'd feel seasick.

Spud It's not going to be like being on a ship, is it?

Fanny What's it gonna be like then?

Spud Like being on a lily-pad.

Fanny Could be quite relaxing actually.

Spud Relaxation comes after . . . in the jacuzzi.

Fanny She's got a *jacuzzi*?

Spud Christina's a posh piece of skirt.

Fanny If she's so posh then what she want with you?

Spud Some slack up her crack and coal in her hole.

Spud and Fanny jump to their feet as the Colonel and Bobbo appear.

Colonel What are you twos doing?

Spud Now?

Colonel Now.

Fanny Right now?

Spud Right fucking –

Fanny Nothing.

Spud Having a break.

Fanny I wouldn't call it a break.

Spud A few moments to rehydrate as instructed by Nurse McKenzie.

Colonel Since when do you take orders from her?

Spud Not an order, just a suggestion from a concerned practitioner.

Colonel She's not even a proper fucking nurse.

Fanny That's no way to talk about Nurse McKenzie.

Spud (*dreamily*) I'd eat her whole damn child just to taste what it came out of. And I'll tell you somert else, she's got the hots for me.

Bobbo Give yer head a shake.

Colonel She's just got engaged to Greenie.

Spud Yeah, but he's an ugly cunt.

Fanny And his cock's a funny shape.

Spud What there is of it.

Fanny Looks like a walnut whip.

Spud Nurse McKenzie deserves more out of life than a walnut whip! I'm telling you now, she may well be engaged but I've not written off the well-rehearsed sick-room scenario.

> *Spud and Fanny role play as Nurse McKenzie (Scots) and Mr Winters.*

Fanny Oooh, hellooo, Mr Winters.

Spud Hello, Nurse McKenzie.

Fanny What can I do for you tayday?

Spud I'm not feeling very well, Nurse.

Fanny What are you doing at work then, when you should be tucked up in bed?

Spud The Colonel said I had to, Nurse.

Fanny (*aghast*) Oooh, that harsh man.

Spud Well, I wouldn't like to criticise the Colonel . . .

Fanny No, no, you're a very loyal worker. But I've had enough run-ins with that man myself to know he has an ego the size of Scotland and a heart just as cold.

> *He puts his hand on Spud's forehead.*

You, however, have a wee temperature.

Spud And a sore throat.

Fanny Sit tight now while I make some notes.

They snap out of role play back to Spud and Fanny.

But beneath the professional concern –

Spud I begin to detect something akin to desire.

Fanny A platonic hand on the shoulder –

Spud Left too long.

Fanny A prolonged glance –

Spud One too many. Enough to suggest . . .

Snap into role play of Mr Winters and Nurse McKenzie.

Fanny Does it hurt anywhere?

Spud nods slowly.

Where does it hurt?

Spud Well . . . (*Sheepishly.*) Several places really.

Fanny I'm going tay have tay do a *full* examination.
Please remove your trooosers!

Spud drops his Y-fronts as Fanny drops to his knees.

Colonel Get these two goons back to work before they
start resuscitating each other's cocks.

Fanny I want a word with you first. Last night at Working
Men's Club.

Colonel What about it?

Fanny A new performer was on. Now we all like a bit of
fun but this was below the belt.

Colonel Why, what happened?

Fanny I will not pay good money to sit there listening to
swearing.

Spud Swearing?

Bobbo (*disgusted*) I don't agree with that.

Fanny If they can't get up there and do a nice clean routine then what's it coming to?

Bobbo And they call themselves artists.

Fanny Filth it was.

Spud No need for it, is there?

Fanny I might as well have come to pit.

Colonel I bet you left, dint you?

Fanny Course I did. I'm not sitting through that with our Lorraine next to me.

Bobbo There's two things the wife's never heard me do in all our years and that's fart and swear. I feel very fucking strongly about both.

Malcom and Jimmy, both bollocksed, appear with their carts.

Colonel Youth, I'll speak to committee, see that you're refunded. What's a matter with youse?

Malcom It's hot.

Fanny Hot?!

Spud Did he just say *hot*?

Colonel (*wipes his brow, shows it*) That's what sweat looks like, youth.

Spud You want to come on to coaling face.

Fanny Ninety degrees.

Spud And that's just on a Monday.

Fanny Come Friday, machinery running all week, it's touching a hundred.

Jimmy We want to come on to face.

Bobbo They want to come on microwave mile.

Jimmy It's what we signed up for, int it? To be miners, not pit ponies. I don't see why you got rid of 'em, I don't.

Colonel (*sarcastically*) Well, it was cruel, wasn't it?

Bobbo What's wrong with yers? You're doing a man's work there.

Spud You're lucky to have any work at all.

Bobbo Bloody right. Plenty of lads out there with none in sight.

Fanny Everybody starts on haulage, youths.

Malcom But do we really have to do it for six months?

Colonel You'll be doing it permanently in a minute.

Bobbo Don't rush to get on face, kid, it's hard graft.

Jimmy Just don't want to do a shit job, that's all.

Fanny There are no shit jobs at pit.

Colonel Every man and every job is important.

Spud That's right.

Bobbo It makes men a' men and the women'll be glad of yer.

Jimmy Glad of us?

Collier Lad

I can hew, girls, I can hack it out
I can hew the coal, I can dance and shout
I can hew, girls, coal so black and fine
I'm a collier lad, working down the mine

It's St Monday's day, and well I do admire
To sit snug at home by my own coal fire
Then it's down to the pub for a pint or two
For to work on Monday would never do

Chorus.

Now my son's fourteen he's a strapping lad
He'll go down the mine just like his dad
And Friday comes we'll pick up our pay
And we'll drink together to round out the day

Chorus.

And it's when I'm dead, oh I know full well
I'll not go to heaven, I'm bound for hell
And my pick and my shovel old Nick he will admire
And he'll set me to hewing coal for his own hellfire

AN APPOINTMENT

Split scene.
  Above: Ian MacGregor, seventy-one years old, big chops.

MacGregor (*to us*) When the American industrialist
Henry Ford first announced his five-dollars-a-day wage,
everybody, that is, everybody in business, thought he was
nuts. It was a hell of a wage back then. It wasn't until
they realised Ford raised wages by cutting down on
manpower through labour-saving technology that
everybody followed suit. Everybody except Britain.
The story of the British disease is of a full-employment
economy, that only managed to stay in the game because
the wages were *so low*. Then came the seventies: an oil
crisis, soaring inflation and wage *rises*. Britain loses its
place in the world markets. The way for you to get it
back is to start shedding jobs. A painful but wholly

necessary change. I'm an industrialist but you can think
of me as the midwife to it.

Below: underground – haulage.
    Fanny and Spud are in the paddy train. Lads are
    digging and knee-deep in a hole.

Spud Who's the lucky ladies?

Malcom (*smitten*) Janice Skevington.

Spud Skevo's daughter? She's got an arse as wide as a
coal bunker.

Fanny It's not the size of the wave that matters but the
motion a' the *ocean*.

Spud So come on then, who's your bride?

Jimmy Mandy. (*Shrugs.*) She's alright, I suppose.

Spud She must be smitten.

Fanny Where did you take 'em?

Malcom We met 'em at bus stop.

Jimmy Stood there talking for a bit.

Malcom Walked it to corner shop.

Jimmy Went down back lane.

Malcom Sat on bridge for a bit.

Jimmy Bought 'em fish and chips.

Malcom We had battered sausages.

Jimmy But we ate 'em back at bus stop.

Malcom By then it was raining.

Beat.

Fanny And you're seeing 'em again, you say?

Malcom (*chuffed*) Saturday night.

Jimmy She's alright, I suppose.

Spud Youths, you're going about it all wrong.

Jimmy We're meeting 'em again, aren't we?

Spud Listen here, I've had more women than you've had hot dinners.

Fanny Mothers and daughters, married and single, old and young: he's mined 'em all.

Spud You need to be impressing the lassies. Taking 'em somewhere different. Giving 'em a reason to get glammed up.

Fanny (*nods*) All women love getting glammed up.

Spud Pub crawl down Mansfield.

Malcom You reckon?

Spud Hit a club as the night draws on. (*Jigs about.*) Get 'em on to dance floor.

Fanny (*nods*) All women love dancing.

Spud Then you've got the bus ride back – top deck.

He demonstrates: yawns, stretches his arm, puts it around Fanny.

You're home and away. Walk her down back lane and knob her.

Fanny He can't knob a lassie down back lane.

Spud Why not? I have. And she thanked me for it.

Fanny My missus' magazine reckons eighty-five per cent of women have faked an orgasm.

Spud Not with me they haven't.

18

Malcom With statistics like that, how do you know?

Fanny You don't. But ninety-nine per cent of men don't give a fuck.

Spud You need to check her heartbeat.

Fanny Her heartbeat?

Spud After you've done it.

Jimmy Why would he do that?

Spud To see if it's beating fast enough. (*Shrugs.*) Her body won't lie to you.

Fanny You've never told me that!

Spud You've never asked. I swear there's been times when I've thought Christina's would bust through one of her ribs, on the other hand I couldn't be sure that the wife was still alive.

Malcom (*confused*) Same man?

Spud Very different women.

Fanny and Spud drive off.

Malcom Do you think she's got a big arse?

Jimmy Well, it's not small, is it?

Malcom Don't matter though, does it?

Jimmy Course it don't. You're not looking at that most a' time, are you?

Malcom Suppose there's somert up with everyone.

Jimmy There's nowt up with her top kit.

Malcom (*grins*) Did you see her dancing last Saturday in that white jumper?

Jimmy Like two kittens playing under a blanket.

They continue shovelling out the hole.

I reckon Spud's right. We take 'em down Mansfield. Bus back. Then down lane.

Malcom Janice int like that.

Jimmy Don't be daft.

Malcom What do you mean?

Jimmy I reckon she's up for it.

Malcom No. She's not.

Jimmy Good thing if you ask me, makes it easier.

Malcom Mandy's one that's putting it about.

Jimmy What you on about?

Malcom (*laughing*) Now who's being daft.

Jimmy goes for Malcom.

Colonel What's going on?!

Colonel appears. Jimmy and Malcom break apart.

What's going on here? (*Beat.*) Right. Out the pit.

Jimmy He started it.

Colonel I don't give a fuck. Both of you out.

Malcom He's right, it was me.

Colonel Don't come all Spartacus on me now, sunshine.

Jimmy But it wasn't my fault!

Colonel (*to Malcom*) Grab him.

Malcom What?

Colonel Grab him now.

Jimmy I haven't done nowt!

Colonel I said grab him.

Jimmy What fucking for –

Malcom violently grabs Jimmy; pulls him towards him.

Colonel (*to Malcom*) You know why you've done that? Because on the face where you're both working, a section of roofing collapsed right where he was standing bringing with it five tonne of rock and earth in less than three fucking seconds. (*Beat.*) Down here, your life is always in another man's hands. Never forget it. (*Beat.*) Now shake fucking hands. If it ever happens again, you'll be sacked on spot.

Up ahead the cage opens; out steps a silhouetted Tilsley. Tilsley is the manager of the pit, but to the men he is God. He wears overalls and a donkey jacket but beneath those a shirt and silk neck scarf; he walks with a metre-long stick. A miner appears, removes Tilsley's donkey jacket for him and hangs it on a hook.

Shit.

Jimmy (*in awe*) Who's that?

Colonel You say nothing.

Malcom (*in awe and panic*) He's coming to us.

Colonel You can say hello, but only if he says it to you.

Malcom Who's –

Colonel And its *Mr* Tilsley.

He walks over to Tilsley.

Morning, Gaffer. I dint know you were coming underground today.

Tilsley I was supposed to have a meeting but I cancelled.

Colonel Has somert happened?

Tilsley Yes, it's pissing it down. Round of golf with some sales twat? Fuck that.

He swings his official's stick as if it were a golf club. A stone flies in the air.

Morning.

Lads Morning . . . Mr Tilsley.

Tilsley (*to Colonel*) Apprentices?

Colonel Been with us three month.

Tilsley How are they?

Colonel Fucking rubbish.

They walk on.

Tilsley I've had word that a new chairman is to be appointed.

Colonel Mr Ezra's leaving Coal Board?

Tilsley Something like that. He was good to us. More than the men know. He was on our side.

Colonel So who are we getting in his place?

Tilsley I haven't been told. (*Beat.*) Uncertain times.

Colonel Aye. And not just for us. (*Beat.*) I best get over to face.

Tilsley I'll join you. How's the heat there?

Colonel Same.

Tilsley And the men?

Colonel There's a job needs doing, they know that. But they shouldn't be working in it.

News
Ian MacGregor has today been named the new chairman of the National Coal Board . . . the man who is credited

with turning round the loss-making steel industry . . .
Labour MPs described the American businessman's
appointment as deeply provocative . . . The Prime Minister
defended her position, saying Ian MacGregor was one of
the most outstanding industrialists in the world with a
reputation for building businesses and creating
employment.

IN THE BALANCE

*In the cage, descending into the pit. The dialogue can be
overlapping.*

Colonel After what he did to British Steel . . .

Bobbo He *halved* the manpower in two years!

Fanny The man's a butcher . . .

Spud Thatcher's henchman . . .

Jimmy He's American, you say?

Bobbo He's here for one thing . . .

Malcom I've never met an American . . .

Fanny What's the union say?

Spud What can they say?

Bobbo What are they gonna do?

Malcom What was that?

Men What?

> *Vooom! The cage drops like a stone down a well. The
> men cry out in terror . . .*

Spud Jesus Christ?!

> *The cage catches and bounces up and down, throwing
> the men about erratically.*

Jimmy What's happening . . .

Fanny Fuck . . .

Colonel Power's gone . . .

Malcom Get me out . . .

Colonel We're alright . . .

Malcom Get me out . . .

Colonel Lamps on . . .

Bobbo It's caught . . .

Colonel We're alright . . .

Bobbo It's stopping . . .

Colonel It's stopping.

The cage's bouncing slows. The men are silent until it comes to a standstill.

Malcom (*panicked*) We're stuck!

Colonel We're fine. Power's tripped.

Bobbo Control room knows we're here.

Jimmy Now what?

Colonel We wait.

Fanny and Spud exchange a glance, minimal.

Malcom We're trapped!

Colonel We're alright. Just, you know . . . keep calm.

Jimmy I think I'm gonna be sick.

Colonel We're alright. (*Beat.*) The wife always said I'd wind up on the end of a rope.

The men laugh a bit then fall silent . . .

Meanwhile – the cage still hanging – above: Peter Walker, politician.

Walker (*to us*) The fate of the government hung by a thread. In 1974 in the middle of an oil crisis the miners held us all to ransom for a pay rise, plunging the country into darkness with their winter strike. Three-day working weeks and a snap general election followed, where we asked you: who governs Britain, us or them? (*Beat.*) We lost. The story of Britain's decline thereafter is one of rampant trade unionism, endless strikes, wage demands, and the people getting bloody well fed up of it. That Margaret came to power ready to take them on became clear to me when she offered me a job: Energy Secretary . . . with a miners' strike.

Walker joins MacGregor.

MacGregor There's no such thing as a free market in energy. Almost all energy resources are *heavily* subsidised, regardless as to whether they are state or privately owned. If energy were truly opened up to a competitive market, we might be sat here like *hippies* talking about renewables.

Walker It was the *amount* of subsidy I was raising.

MacGregor Britain receives the lowest subsidy per tonne of coal of all the common market countries. Hell, in the US coal gets almost as much subsidy as oil does. And it's not even hard to extract: they're bulldozing into a mountain half the time.

Walker (*tight smile*) As Minister of Energy I am aware of the global levels of subsidy.

MacGregor Sure you are. I'm just letting you know that it's a pretty tough hand you want me to play, if you want to cut competitive subsidy and still have competitive coal.

Walker What we want is to stem the losses. We're not expecting a genie out of bottle.

MacGregor That I can do. The nub of the problem: over-production and high-cost pits. Let's start with the former. For the last two years production has been allowed to run free.

Walker We've been stockpiling for a strike. (*Beat.*) Any attempts to improve the industry will be met with resistance. We thought it prudent to prepare.

MacGregor And financially it's crippled the industry. From now on we will produce only as much coal as we can use. High-cost pits, those where the coal is hard to extract, have got to go. There's your drain on the taxpayer's purse. And I'm ready, having had a good look around, to start cutting out some of our other dead wood.

Walker (*beams*) And that's exactly what we want, Ian.

MacGregor Bureaucrats.

Walker Bureaucrats?

MacGregor Dead wood. That goes for staff in your department too.

Walker That's perhaps something that could be looked at further down the line.

MacGregor If it's a business you want and not a government department, I say we look at it now.

Walker If there is some restructuring to be done –

MacGregor I have a vast army of people over at Whitehall on *my* payroll.

Walker I'm not sure that tackling that issue now would have a significant impact.

MacGregor Are you kidding me? It would be a major saving. I'm going to be doing it at the Coal Board, I'm getting rid of half the staff!

Walker Interesting . . . Well, with regard to *my* department, I'll certainly have a look at that.

MacGregor I want to say that none of the problems we're facing are insurmountable. British Coal is *not* British Steel. It's a resource. Rises in oil prices will inevitably expand the market for coal and with the right investment we can enlarge that market even more. (*Lights a cigar.*) You know, Peter, reason I got into this business in the first place: there's a future.

Below: the cage still hanging, the men sweating.

Fanny My balls are on fire.

Spud You got nappy rash?

Fanny I've had it since last week. Need to get some cream for it.

Spud What better reason to go and see Nurse McKenzie! Oooh hellooo, Mr Fannshore.

Fanny Hello, Nurse McKenzie.

Spud What can I do for you tay day?

Fanny I've got a heat rash, Nurse.

Spud (*aghast*) So what are you doing working in ninety degreeeees?

Fanny The Colonel says I have to, Nurse.

Spud Oooh, that harsh man. Tell me, Mr Fannshore, where does it hurt *this* time?

Fanny (*sheepishly.*) Well. Two places really.

Spud Would you be wanting some cream for those two places?

Fanny nods.

Would you be wanting Nurse McKenzie to slather it on?

They laugh. A sound, everyone is silent, then the whirring starts.

Bobbo Just in the nick of time.

They laugh with relief as the cage descends.

Pit bottom: They step and proceed forwards, except for Malcom who is silent.

Malcom I want to go back up.

Colonel No you don't.

Malcom I do. I need to go up for a bit.

Colonel If you go up now, kid, you won't come back down.

Bobbo Like falling off a bike, you've got get back on.

Fanny Otherwise you start to fear it.

Malcom looks at the men, at Jimmy, then turns and walks towards the cage.

Jimmy I'm coming with you.

Colonel You stay where you are.

Malcom I don't want you to come.

Colonel Don't worry, he's not.

Jimmy I'm not coming back down . . .

Colonel Hold on a minute . . .

Jimmy Unless you're with me. (*Beat.*) What's it gonna be?

Malcom I think we should stay.

Jimmy Alright then.

Malcom We're staying.

A deep intestinal rumble . . . louder . . . louder still . . . now blaring, grinding, heaving . . .

THE FACE

A huge, menacing steel structure edges forwards; thick dust spews out, blue liquid light exhales from the machinery and cuts through the dark, a cutter mounts the seam wall, coal and earth collapsing in its wake; a conveyor runs along the floor catching and zooming off each load. A thickly linked convict-like iron chain runs across the length of the face; buckling, threatening to unleash. This is the coaling face. Malcom and Jimmy stand still, daunted by what's before them.

Spud comes to a stop with the cutter as Malcom, Jimmy and the Colonel appear.

Colonel What we doing, youth, cutting slack or coal? 'Cause what's coming off here looks like a fucking slag heap.

Spud gets back to the cutter.

It's the skill of the driver that gets as little dirt as possible and the maximum amount of coal so he constantly has to judge the horizon – (*Indicates.*) The band where the coal is thickest. We don't get paid for muck.

Fanny is nearby, operating the chocks.

These steel chocks are what replaced the timber props and keep the roof up. Course it still comes down.

Jimmy How often?

Colonel Every week.

Malcom What do you do?

Colonel Get out the way.

Fanny (*shouts*) Loading!

They walk on towards Bobbo who is building what look like timber pillars.

Colonel Bobbo's putting up more support with timber and steel because the roofing at the ends of the face are the most vulnerable.

Jimmy Where's this water come from?

Colonel The lake.

Malcom We're under a lake?

Colonel This is nothing, over-your-boots water. You can be working up to your waist in it.

Malcom Quite somert to think there's a lake up there.

Colonel There's two hundred and fifty million years up there. Way I see it, a miner, he's not just working a piece of rock he's working with the world.

Bobbo 'He putteth forth his hand upon the flinty rock. He overturneth the mountains by the roots. He cutteth out rivers among the rocks, and his eyes . . . his eyes seeth every precious thing. He bindeth the streams that they weep not. And the thing that is hidden he bringeth forth to light.' From the Bible that.

Malcom It's lovely.

Jimmy 'Tis, int it.

Colonel God . . . was a miner.

They laugh. Suddenly –

Fanny (*shouts*) Sheds in!

*Vooom! They dive forwards, several tonnes collapses,
thick dust everywhere . . .*
   *A deep, eerie exhale of the pit, the creak and groan
of the roofing.*
   *Two lamp lights beam upwards through the crater-
like hole now gaping open from the roofing; it extends
upwards some twenty feet. A continuous stream of
bitting trickles down, heightening the sense of danger
and vulnerability of the men now assessing the
damage. Spud is crouched on the ground, his head
lamp angled upwards; the Colonel is standing on top
of the chocks (the steel structure) looking into the
cavity. Fanny is on the ground close by the Colonel.
The lads and Bobbo are well clear of it to one side.*

Fanny How high is it?

Colonel Well, let's put me it this way, I can see dinosaur
shit.

Spud Ah fuck.

Malcom What does that mean?

Bobbo We're doing overtime.

Colonel It's about twenty foot.

Fanny and Spud exchange a look, minimal.

Alright then, let's get up the bastard.

*Their positions remain the same but Fanny now passes
timber blocks to the Colonel.*

Malcom What they gonna do?

Bobbo Climb up and pack it with timber support so as it
don't fall down.

Jimmy How they gonna get up it if it's twenty foot high?

Bobbo They build scaffolding at the same time as putting up the support.

Malcom That's what Fanny and Colonel's doing?

Bobbo And Spud's spotting. It's the spotter's job to look out for it giving way.

Jimmy But there's stuff falling out from it now.

Bobbo That's just bitting, you always get that. He's watching for the big stuff.

Malcom What's the big stuff?

Bobbo The whole lot collapsing.

Jimmy But the spotter stops that from happening?

Bobbo If he spots it in time, aye. He calls it out and you jump down out way.

Malcom But what if you're one that's working really high up?

Bobbo Then you can't just jump down, you need to make sure you've got an escape route.

Jimmy What's your escape route?

Bobbo It's . . . complicated.

Malcom So whose job is it to climb up to top?

Bobbo Colonel will be one of 'em. It's not his job. But he'll be going up.

Jimmy Why's he doing it if it's not his job?

Bobbo I once asked him that. He said to me it's a bit like General Custer, when him and his men were surrounded by all them Sioux Indians in Big Horn. He thought it was his duty to stand there with his men prepared to do same as 'em. Prepared to die with 'em.

The work continues in dim light – the men climbing higher, the danger mounting.

SCARED PEOPLE

Above: MacGregor's office.

MacGregor I should perhaps tell you this now, Peter. I once spent a week at a psychiatry clinic in Kansas at the urging of my boss, Bud Burstein. He figured that it was a priority for top government and us executives to see head shrinkers. After all, we are the guys who have to understand not just the motivations of our own but those of others too. So I went, somewhat sceptical, and had a shattering experience.

Walker Right.

MacGregor I now have an understanding of the mechanics of people's behaviour. And that includes the lowest common denominator: the working man. In the short time that I've been chairman of the Coal Board I have come to realise that miners are motivated in the earning of good money.

Walker Well, yes, undoubtedly.

MacGregor And *not* in going out on strike.

Walker Forgive me, but announcing the closure of twenty pits –

MacGregor High-cost pits!

Walker But pits all the same, will almost certainly prompt some form of strike action.

MacGregor Non-profitable pits have been shut down in the past.

Walker That was before Arthur Scargill became president of their union.

MacGregor I met him last week – articulate enough, but all trade unionists strike me the same.

Walker (*alarm*) No, no, he's different. He's not to be treated as just another trade unionist.

MacGregor But the union doesn't determine a strike, the workers do.

Walker He has *immense* influence over them. You have his file, he's a *Marxist*, he's –

MacGregor I don't think the men have the stomach for it. These are different times.

Walker I believe our strategy ought to assume that they will strike because the only way we can win is by pre-empting one. That way we have it at the time of our choosing. We need to get through this winter, of course.

MacGregor You're proposing we announce the first wave of closures next spring?

Walker Yes. Until then we focus our efforts on keeping the morale up across the coal fields.

MacGregor I've been working my way through the pits, getting to know the managers and meeting some of the men.

Walker I think that's hugely important.

MacGregor I want them to know I'm a general who leads from the trenches.

Walker Speak to the men directly, reassure them about the future.

MacGregor I've told everybody the same thing, I believe there are many normal working miners out there who are prepared to accept that the world no longer owes them a living and that a day of reckoning is bound to come. If they want a living they have to earn it.

Pause.

Walker I think we should confer and agree on exactly what we say.

MacGregor Peter, everyone knows I'm here to put things right.

Walker The closures are going to be a very sensitive issue.

MacGregor And a simple one: men in failing pits are no longer entitled to the taxpayers' purse.

Walker When we do announce the closures it will be my job to present the case for them. The argument has to be, and of course *is*, purely economical.

MacGregor You bet it is – this industry's looking at a two hundred and fifty million pound loss for the year.

Walker Exactly, and that's all we need to say, anything else – well, it's like toothpaste, awfully tricky to get back into the tube once it's out. We have to have the public on our side.

MacGregor What will get the public on side is some economic sanity.

Walker Yes, but the public are fond of the miners. They are regarded as the backbone of the old working class, they are respected across classes –

MacGregor I don't like class distinctions. Americans waste no time on them. Anybody can be anybody, as long as they put the work in and are reasonably self-confident. It doesn't matter to me if a man's father was a cow puncher or a millionaire.

Walker But back to Britain, back to the miners, who *are* very class conscious.

MacGregor Why would anybody want to limit themselves like that?

Walker My point is this, people are angry. Brixton, Toxteth, the anger . . . the violence – riots of a kind we haven't seen in this country. We haven't seen a collapse in industrial production like this since 1921. And it's not just industry – businesses continue to close, firm after firm folds. The cuts in public spending are set to continue. Unemployment is up by another million. We now have three million unemployed! That's one in eight people. That was once . . . unimaginable.

MacGregor It is an assumption of government that high unemployment results in an angry people. But coming from business, I see it somewhat differently. High unemployment doesn't make people angry, it makes them scared. (*Smiles.*) And scared people don't risk losing their jobs.

PITMAN POLITICS

Underground: coaling face.
  Snap break. Fanny and Bobbo are sat eating their snap. Jimmy and Malcom are joining them with their shovels still in hand when Spud appears.

Spud Give us your shovel.

  Jimmy does so. Spud goes to Fanny, who has a plastic bag on his knees for his cobs.

Pass us your bag.

Fanny I've not finished me cobs yet.

Spud I need a bag, Fanny.

Fanny But it's me tablecloth for me cobs!

Spud I need a shit *now*.

Fanny hands over the bag and Spud runs off with the shovel. Colonel appears.

Colonel Where's Spud off now?

Bobbo For a shit.

Fanny Do you mind?

Bobbo Sorry, I dint know we were sat at table.

Fanny Argh, what?!

Bobbo Now bloody what?!

Fanny She's put tuna in one of me cobs.

They laugh at Fanny. Head lamps cut through the dark up ahead.

Jimmy Mr Tilsley's here.

Malcom He's not on his own either.

The Colonel walks over to Tilsley. Bishop is flanked by two men with clipboards.

Colonel What's going on, Gaffer?

Tilsley Mr Bishop and his associates are from the Coal Board.

Colonel I wasn't told nowt about it.

Tilsley Neither was I. Mr MacGregor's paying us a visit next week, Mr Bishop's here to have a look around.

Colonel *MacGregor?*

Bishop Mr Tilsley?

Tilsley It's nothing to worry about. Yes, Mr Bishop?

Bishop What on earth are we to do about this heat?

Tilsley Yes, it's been very demanding on the men.

Bishop You must install a water cooler.

Tilsley That er . . . can be arranged.

As there are no toilets underground the idea of a water cooler is absurd.

Bishop How many are in the canteen?

Tilsley Water coolers? None.

Bishop Do you have one in your office?

Tilsley Yes.

Bishop Marvellous! Well, see that it's brought down. It's just for Mr MacGregor's visit.

Bishop now clocks Colonel, specifically his ponytail, today sporting a pink ribbon.

Good gosh, Mr Tilsley, what have we got here?

Tilsley Ah yes, our Deputy –

Bishop An *official* with that *hair*?

Tilsley Don't be fooled now, Mr Bishop, by Tony's appearance. Thirty years of experience –

Bishop Yes, yes. You do of course realise that when Mr MacGregor comes you will have to do something about . . . (*points his clipboard at Colonel's ponytail*) *that*?

Colonel I do, yeah. I'll be putting two ribbons in it instead a one.

Tilsley leads Bishop and his associates off.

Tilsley Fantastic miner. One of the best men I've got.

Bishop But where's the respect, Mr Tilsley?

Spud When's MacGregor coming?

Colonel Next week.

Bobbo Ian Butcher MacGregor.

Fanny We don't know that, youth.

Bobbo Who don't? They want to privatise, I tell you that now.

Colonel Our fathers would turn over in their graves.

Bobbo Industry being decimated all around us. Not be too long before they come after us.

Spud We've had thirty men die in pits this year.

Fanny Fuck's sake, Spud.

Spud I'm saying imagine how many it would be if we were back in private hands?

Colonel I don't see it happening.

Fanny Not after '74 we won't.

Bobbo We should have kept Heath in – better than Maggie, wasn't he, lads?

Jimmy (*shrugs*) I'm not interested in politics.

Bobbo Not interested in *politics*?

Colonel It's not politics, its pitman politics.

Bobbo How do you think you're sat here now, youths?

Malcom What do you mean?

Bobbo Eating your snap?

Jimmy 'Cause its snap time.

Bobbo *Sixty years*. Sixty years our men fought for you to have a snap time.

Jimmy And they only got us twenty minutes?

Colonel Cheeky bugger.

Bobbo Everything we have, somewhere down line, somebody's had to put up a fight for it.

Fanny Without our union we'd still be earning nowt.

Bobbo And if you don't know that, what we've had to fight for. You'll let 'em take it back.

Blackleg Miner

Well it's in the evening after dark
When the blackleg miner creeps to work
With his moleskin pants and dirty shirt
There goes the blackleg miner!

Well he takes his tools and down he goes
To hew the coal that lies below
There's not a woman in this town-row
Will look at the blackleg miner.

Oh, Seghill is a terrible place
They rub wet clay in the blackleg's face
And around the heaps they run a foot race
To catch the blackleg miner!

So don't go near the Delaval mine
Across the way they stretch a line
To catch the throat and break the spine
Of the dirty blackleg miner.

They grab his duds and his pick as well
And hide them down the pit of hell
Down ye go, and fare ye well
You dirty blackleg miner!

So join the union while you may
Don't wait until your dying day
For that may not be far away
You dirty blackleg miner!

THE RIDLEY PLAN

*Nicholas Ridley: chain smoker, Coward-like drawl,
amused smirk, dishevelled.*

Ridley (*to us*) What a heavenly summer. The economy's
in ruins, unemployment's through the roof, but *finally* we
have proved to those wets in the Party that not only can
we do something naughty and get away with it, we can
be re-elected to do it all over again with a huge majority.
The once unthinkable privatisation is on the horizon,
nothing stands in our way, nothing . . . but the unions.
I have with me here a report, it's causing quite a stir,
though I can hardly see why. I've merely set out in
writing what we're all thinking: the miners must be
beaten. And I know how to do it. I have a plan . . . the
Ridley Plan.

> *Walker and MacGregor have reached the end of their
> reports.*

In the end it boils down to this: keeping the lights on.
They go out, we lose. Presently, you have the stockpiles
of coal at the pitheads, I advise you to start moving it to
the power stations from now whilst we can still get at it.

MacGregor Power stations don't have that storage
capacity.

Ridley We've been quietly purchasing land next to them
for that very reason. We've also encouraged private
companies to employ non-union road hauliers for the
movement of coal. The discreet conversion of coal-fired

power stations to dual-firing is almost complete, giving us the option of burning oil instead of coal should our stocks become exhausted. (*Flicks report.*) The National Riot Squad I've already covered, in effect our third force: somewhere between the army and the police. Ah yes, *benefits.* We cut off the money supply with the withdrawal of benefits. Strikers have never been able to claim for themselves but in the past their dependants have. The take-up has always been very low, I'll grant them that, but in the event of a long strike I'm confident they would claim if the option were there.

MacGregor Well, Nick, you know a what a maxim of mine is? Always get your ducks lined up.

Ridley We have been rearming as if facing the threat of Hitler.

Walker The union are making preparations of their own. Scargill's called an overtime ban.

Ridley (*amused*) The cloth-capped colonels are finally readying themselves for the last war.

MacGregor He's going to run the ban through the winter, start hardening the attitude of the men.

Walker It will put a dent in our coal stocks.

MacGregor (*dismissive*) There's enough to see through a six-month strike.

Walker That's assuming it would be over before then.

MacGregor Fourteen weeks. It'll be over in *fourteen weeks.*

Walker I think that's hugely –

MacGregor Soon as their money runs out they'll be back, same as British Steel.

Walker I really think it's a mistake to compare –

MacGregor You mark my words.

Ridley However long it takes, gentlemen, however long. Remember Drake's dispatch to Walsingham. 'There must be a beginning of any great matter, but the continuing unto the end until it be thoroughly finished yields the true glory.' For forty years we've been held back by the unions but their reign is almost over. No more beer and beef sandwiches at Number Ten. Break the miners' union, break them all.

MacGregor It amazes me they've been allowed to gain such power in the first place.

Ridley It is most extraordinary that an organisation, essentially a babushka in a headscarf, has outmanoeuvred a number of Conservatives . . . (*Looks at Walker.*)

Walker It's hardly through cunning, they control the energy supply.

Ridley The pitmen were allowed to grow too big for their pit boots.

Walker I think we're done here. Unless there's anything else, I'm going to head off.

Ridley What those men need is a good dose of the real world. Enough of their featherbedding. Competition, competition. (*To MacGregor.*) Wouldn't you say?

Walker I hardly think now's the time to talk about that. Even the suggestion of privatising would clearly work against us.

Ridley It's not because you're against it? (*To MacGregor.*) Our views are so very often different. Peter once asked me, knowing I like to paint and draw, whether I should like to be Minister of the *Arts*. I actually had to explain to him that the Ministry of Arts should not even exist.

Walker Nick forgets, of course – he wasn't even a minister at the time – it was me who actually began privatising.

Ridley That's right. You denationalised a travel agent's and a pub.

Walker It was a string of pubs.

Ridley Four.

Walker My point is I've long recognised the weaknesses of state ownership.

Ridley Then what could be better than the jewel of Attlee's crown, coal?

MacGregor I've always said government has no business being in business. I share your frustrations.

Walker Yes, well, there is the small matter of Britain's energy future to consider.

Ridley We have: it's called diversification. In other words freedom from the miners' blackmail.

Walker If you think Arthur Scargill is the only energy tsar you really ought to visit the Middle East.

Ridley I think a job for life in an overmanned industry paid for by the taxpayer is over.

Walker And I think you're stepping well beyond your brief, Transport Secretary.

Ridley We're having an exchange of ideas. Ones the rest of the Cabinet share.

Walker As usual we agree on the problems. I don't always share your view on the solutions.

Ridley Sorry, I always forget what yours are.

Walker Those with privilege and power have responsibilities.

Ridley Ah yes, one-nation Toryism: the rich mucking in. How noble.

Walker I don't see why wanting a decent life for everyone should be mocked.

Ridley Thatcher's Britain is people empowering themselves.

Walker Is unemployment empowering?

Ridley Unemployment is evidence of the progress we're making.

MacGregor Painful but necessary.

Ridley When we hear people squeal, we know that what we are doing is right.

Walker Is that what you tell the three million unemployed?

Ridley Three million, yet for the life of me I can't find just one to paint the gates of my home.

Walker Within *five years* almost a *third* of manufacturing has vanished from our shores.

Ridley If it went to the wall it was ripe for the kill anyway.

Walker Oh, come off it. Surely you can do better than that.

Ridley This government, and therefore the taxpayer, is not going to bail out bankrupt firms or nationalise them or give them money to tide them over. Those days are gone. It's sink or swim. The fittest will of course survive.

Walker But you've made it impossible for manufacturing. Exchange controls abolished, hiked-up interest rates –

Ridley Manufacturing's low grade, leave it to China.

Walker Do you think Switzerland's just banking and services? It's one of the most industrialised economies in the world. And so were we.

Ridley We aren't renewing the economy.

Walker I can see that.

Ridley We're reinventing it!

Walker From the text books of economists! But economists are not politicians.

Ridley Economists are politicians, they just don't have to be elected.

Milton Friedman appears.

Milton (*to us*) To reinvent the economy you need a truly free market and a truly free market requires a free and flexible labour market. Problem is, half of all the workers in this country are not free. They are trade unionists. The way to tackle the union problem is unemployment. Zero unemployment is highly undesirable in a free market anyway, as when the unemployment level drops there is an upward surge in wages. I prefer to use the term *natural rate of unemployment*. But the way to solve the union problem is *high* unemployment. To deepen a recession. More specifically, to deepen a recession for industries where organised labour is strongest. High unemployment will break that strength and if necessary a defining confrontation with a union will prove it. Only then will you have the opportunity to restructure nationalised industries and public services unrestrained, to make them attractive assets, to pave the way to the new frontier . . . privatisation. Privatisation will not only make investment bankers rich, it will transform the stock market and therefore the financial sector by adding massively to the amount of capital held in the form of shares. The more shares there are, the more liquid the market becomes, as there's more and more to buy and sell. And then, ladies and gentleman, then you need to get out of its way because a truly free market is an unregulated market. From then on, what will be possible is what the Prime Minister herself says is impossible: money . . . for nothing.

COOL WATER

Underground: coaling face.
    The water-cooler glows brilliantly; appears almost magical.

Fanny It's great, int it?

Spud I want one of these babies at home.

Fanny You could fill it with beer.

Bobbo It's in the bloody way if you ask me.

Spud Come on, Bobbo. You've got try it.

Fanny Don't use your flask!

Bobbo Why not?

Fanny There's cups.

Bobbo What difference does it make?

Fanny The cups come with it.

    Bobbo uses his flask anyway.

There's always one who's got spoil it.

Malcom It does taste different though.

Bobbo Course it bloody don't.

Jimmy I hope we get to keep it.

Fanny This is the life, eh, lads?

Spud This is the life of professionals. This is what they do *all* day. Sip cool water.

MacGregor appears with Tilsley and Colonel. Bishop trails behind.

You should go over, introduce yourself.

Bobbo I'm not shaking his hand.

Malcom I've never met an American.

Fanny He's Scottish, actually.

Malcom *Scottish?*

Fanny What's up with Scottish?

MacGregor How's the roofing up there?

Colonel It's gonna give us problems.

MacGregor I bet the damn flooring will too.

Colonel You could say that.

They laugh a little. MacGregor coughs. Spud pours a cup of water from the cooler.

MacGregor Thank you. Well it's good to be here. I wanted to introduce myself to you men. I know there's been some unrest in the coalfields recently. I regret that. I regret anything that undermines the spirit of the industry. So let me be clear, I have no intention of running this industry down. Far from it. I want to make investments. I want to expand the market for coal. I want us to pioneer clean coal. And I want to wake up what I call our sleeping giants: pits with huge reserves such as this. Back in the US, I ran a mining company for many years, watched it grow from zero to profit. Now it's my job to sell the coal, yours to mine it. And I have every faith in your ability to do that. British miners are considered to be, and rightly so, the most skilled in the world. I've visited some mines in my time – Russian, South African, Australian, Polish – and there's always British miners in them – face men, development men, surveyors, managers. Course, I'd rather us export our coal than our men. I want us to work together to do that.

MacGregor and his convoy leave. The Colonel follows with Tilsley.

Spud The Yanks . . . they've just got it. They've just fucking got it.

Fanny They could all be movie stars.

Spud Comes naturally to 'em, don't it?

Bobbo You were so far up his arsehole.

Spud You stand need talking. 'I'm not shaking his hand.'

Bobbo I dint want to make a scene, that's all.

Fanny Sounded positive, dint it.

Bobbo Don't believe any of it.

Spud Sounded alright.

Bobbo What do you think an overtime ban's for?

Malcom and Jimmy are on the shovel with Colonel overseeing.

Malcom It was great what he said about pits. That we've all a future.

Colonel That don't mean youse have got one in 'em. Not if yers are shovelling like that.

Jimmy Why, what's up?

Colonel Shovelling's not just slinging dirt and coal, you know? (*Demonstrates.*) You've got to keep your shoulders

49

in line with the movement of the shovel. Get your whole weight behind that swing. Push the shovel with the weight of your knee. Your forward hand guides the shovel and moves right to the blade. The handle is dropped to loosen the load and your forward hand takes the weight into the swing.

Colonel stops his demonstration. Jimmy and Malcom try again.

Better. But there's something else you have to put into shovelling 'cause after four hours of that you're gonna be bollocksed and you've got another four hours ahead of you. And there's only one thing that'll keep you going. And that . . . is *pride*. When you stand before that wall of coal with the task of shovelling two tonne off of it, you think of the men that have done it before you.

They shovel. Miners cast in silhouette stand behind: past and present merge.

Your brother!

Malcom casts back to the man behind, who in turn casts back to the man behind him.

Your father!

Jimmy casts back to the man behind him and so on.

Your grandfather!

They are now shovelling furiously.

That's it, youths! That's it! Show yersens to be a worker!

They are now working so fast they advance ahead of their predecessors until, exhausted but exhilarated, they throw down their shovels. A choreographed climactic-movement sequence perhaps follows that shows the lads are no longer apprentices.

CORTONWOOD

Underground: coaling face, months later. Jimmy rushes on.

Jimmy Cortonwood Colliery's being shut!

Fanny What?

Spud Cortonwood?

Fanny Where's that?

Bobbo Yorkshire, int it?

Jimmy South Yorkshire. They've gone out on strike.

Colonel Where d'you hear that?

Jimmy Benton just told me.

Colonel How does he know?

Jimmy He overheard Tilsley talking about it.

Fanny Benton's bone idle.

Spud Don't mean he's deaf though, does it? Why's it being shut?

Jimmy He don't know.

Bobbo Bloody provocation is what.

Pause.

Colonel Come on then, let's finish this. I'm gonna call control room, see where Malc is.

Spud Is he back today?

Jimmy Supposed to be.

Fanny He is. I seen him down street yesterday.

Colonel That reminds me, I seen Flinty from pit top in Club last night. Told me he's got Parkinson's.

Spud Parkinson's?

Bobbo He's only been retired two months.

Fanny What do you say to that, eh?

Colonel I said better that than Alzheimer's, youth. You'd rather spill your pint than not know where you've put it.

Jimmy Here he is!

Raucous noises from the men as Malcom appears. All the men shake hands with a beaming Malcom and offer their congratulations.

Colonel So, er, are you alright about it?

Malcom How do you mean?

Colonel Baby being a girl.

Malcom (*baffled*) Well, yeah, she's lovely.

Colonel That's all that matters then.

Bobbo Course it is.

Colonel You can always go in for another.

Bobbo Course he can.

They give Malcom an extra consolatory slap on the back and continue rigging.

Spud Don't worry about it.

Malcom But . . . I'm not.

Spud (*grinning*) It takes a big man to sire girls.

Jimmy How's your Janice doing?

Malcom She's good. Today's first time she'll be alone with baby.

Jimmy She'll be right.

Malcom Mrs Perkins from next door's gonna pop round and see if she needs any help.

Jimmy I say, you heard news this morning?

Malcom What's that?

Jimmy They're closing a South Yorkshire pit, they've gone out on strike.

Malcom No. (*Beat.*) No, I dint hear that.

Colonel (*shouts*) Firing!

They cover their ears – dynamite sets off a series of explosions, smoke everywhere.

Above: MacGregor's office – MacGregor is at his desk. Walker stands, fuming.

Walker How did this happen? How the hell did this happen?

MacGregor George Hayes, the South Yorkshire Coal Board director, went and told Jack Taylor –

Walker Who's Jack Taylor?

MacGregor He's a Yorkshire union man – in a meeting that Cortonwood Colliery would close.

Walker Why?! Why did he tell him that?

MacGregor He misunderstood his instructions and jumped the gun.

Walker Jumped the gun? Cortonwood is *not even on our closure list*.

MacGregor I don't know where in the hell he got it from.

Walker Do you think he said it on purpose . . . sabotage?

MacGregor I wouldn't say that announcing the closure of one pit sabotages anything for us.

Walker He got the wrong pit, for Christ's sake.

MacGregor Given the choice I'd've kept it open.

Walker We've had no closure review there. This summer we spent one million pounds improving their washery. Hundreds of men have just transferred there from another pit having been promised a future.

MacGregor I didn't guarantee them more than five years.

Walker And now they've been told they have five weeks!

MacGregor Look, I know that in procedural terms George got it wrong.

Walker And to top it all it's in South Yorkshire. The *heartland*.

MacGregor But we gotta stick to shutting it now or we lose face.

Walker I've already lost face.

MacGregor Peter, five days from now we will announce the closure of twenty pits nationally.

Walker But our plan was to announce them *all* on the same day.

MacGregor I'm not sure what the problem is here.

Walker The problem . . .?

MacGregor We throw down the gauntlet, they will have a ballot and they will vote *not* to strike.

Walker A strike is already under way. That's the problem.

News

Ian MacGregor, Chairman of the National Coal Board, has announced today that twenty uneconomic pits will have to close, putting twenty thousand miners out of work. As anger flared across the coalfields, the industrial tycoon warned that coal had been stockpiled in readiness for a prolonged stoppage with walk-outs sweeping through the Yorkshire area.

Underground: new coaling face.
The men are doing the new get-in for a face – lots of activity, with focus shifting between the men. Jimmy and Malcom are setting timber blocks over the chocks up to the roof.

Jimmy Scargill was right all along, he said they had a secret hit-list of pits. Pass a block. Uneconomic. It's bollocks. Cortonwood's got best coal in Yorkshire.

Malcom I know, Jimmy, I know.

Jimmy What's up with you?

Malcom Nowt.

Jimmy Not ideal timing, is it?

Malcom Can we talk about somert else?

Jimmy What's your Janice say?

Malcom She's worried. She keeps watching news, listening to radio.

Jimmy But what she say?

Malcom She don't want me out on strike.

Jimmy Make her see it's not just twenty pits at stake, it's whole industry.

Malcom She's asked me to vote not to, Jimmy.

Jimmy stops what he's doing and stares long and hard at Malcom. Colonel appears.

Colonel Are yous about done? I don't want to leave it for next shift.

Jimmy Just about. Pass us a block. (*Beat.*) Malc, pass us a block.

Colonel What's up with you?

Malcom Nowt. Bit tired.

Colonel Baby playing up, is it?

Malcom I'm helping with the night feeds.

Colonel You're not, are you?

Malcom Our Janice is not breast-feeding no more, so.

Colonel That's your biggest mistake. You want to keep it on the tit as long as you can, youth.

Spud, Fanny and Bobbo are putting their pit clothes back on, having finished up.

Fanny I'm up to my knackers in it. New car. No overtime.

Spud I'm still paying off that miserable bow-legged cow.

Bobbo Would that be the mother of your children?

Spud If you'd had a divorce you'd know the answer to that.

Fanny I promised our Lorraine a holiday abroad this summer.

Bobbo I don't know why, bloody obvious this was coming. I could've told you that.

Spud And you have, many times.

Fanny Twenty thousand jobs. Poor bastards.

Bobbo Don't give 'em your sympathy, give 'em your vote.

Tilsley joins the Colonel.

Colonel Good morning.

Tilsley Is it fuck. Where are we at?

Colonel Next shift can get straight into seam. What's time-frame for this one, Gaffer?

Tilsley Eight months. That was the plan anyway.

Colonel We should be alright with that.

Tilsley You haven't heard, have you?

Colonel What's that?

Tilsley Scargill's announced a national strike.

Colonel National strike?

The men stop their blather.

Tilsley Just over an hour ago.

Fanny What's this?

Colonel says nothing. Men look to Tilsley.

Spud What's going on?

Tilsley A national strike has been sanctioned by the national executive under Rule 41.

Spud What? What rule?

Tilsley It allows areas to strike without calling a ballot. You've not heard of it because it's bollocks. It's unconstitutional. And suicide. They have coal stocks. Summer's on its way. You do not want to go head-on with this government. Not this time. I'm telling you now, she will make an example of us all. So if Scargill doesn't want to see our industry run into the ground, he needs to start acting like a politician. And that means compromise, selling out, whatever you want to call it. When a ship is at risk of sinking, when the water is pouring in, the captain orders the necessary hatches *to be shut*! And those men perish. But the rest . . . the rest will survive.

Tilsley leaves. Spud breaks the silence.

Spud There can't be a national strike without a national ballot.

Jimmy Half the coalfields are already out.

Bobbo The men have voted with their feet.

Spud That's not the same as having a ballot.

Fanny The men have always had their say.

Bobbo We've never agreed on a bloody ballot yet.

Spud There's never been a national strike without one.

Jimmy Previous strikes have been over pay and conditions, which affects everybody.

Malcom So does going out on strike.

Bobbo You're right there, it's not about pay, it's about saving jobs.

Colonel Scargill should call a ballot.

Bobbo Scargill's one man.

Spud He's the head of the union.

Bobbo He hasn't decided it, the men have.

Spud Yorkshire has, we haven't.

Fanny It's not just Yorkshire, Scotland's out, and Kent . . .

Malcom And there's areas that are not – Derbyshire, Leicestershire, Wales . . .

Spud If a ballot says we strike then we fucking strike, tough tittie if you voted not to.

Bobbo Funny no one said that in '76.

Fanny (*rolls eyes*) Here we go.

Jimmy Look, we're already *on* strike.

Malcom No we're not.

Fanny This is why we should have a ballot.

Spud But Scargill don't know if he can get a yes vote with one so he's not asking us at all.

Bobbo Half the coalfields out.

Spud Half of us aren't.

Jimmy They're gonna come picketing now.

Spud They can stand there and picket all they like, I'm not striking until I've had my vote.

Fanny You can't scab, Spud.

Spud Scab?

Colonel Come on then, let's get showered.

Spud No, hang on a minute.

Fanny You know how it goes. You come out 'cause of your mates.

Spud Mate? My mate's calling me a scab.

Fanny Get used to it. That's what you're gonna be hearing.

Colonel I say, that's enough.

Spud You best get him away from me.

Colonel I said that's enough.

Fanny I'm not gonna be nowhere near you.

Colonel ENOUGH! You have a problem, you take it up top 'cause it don't happen down here! (*Beat.*) It's hot. (*Beat.*) Everybody's hot.

The men, clearly shaken, disperse. Stand thinking alone.

Water sprinkles down. One by one they begin to undress.

Each soaps the back of the man beside him, Fanny will wash Spud's and vice versa.

End of Act One.

Act Two

Bang! The sound of an exhaust firing. A motorbike with a sidecar drives in at speed. It brakes. Out from the sidecar pops a Yorkshire picket: helmet, goggles, tats, cans.

Picket 1 (*to us*) Ow doo, lads? Tha's all having an early ride today? Well, ger on back to your lasses' bones, cos the pit's on *strike*!

Pickets from around the country appear and make their case to us.

A pit village is just that. A village way a pit and nothing else. If we lose that what hay we got? What hay we been offered tay replace it?

Picket 2 Thousand-quid redundancy for every year service. What that buy 'em?

Picket 3 I don't want my two bairns doon pit, if they can get somert better. But there's no shame in pit. It's an honourable job. An apprenticeship worth fighting for.

Picket 4 This government is not just anti-coal. It's anti-*nationalised* coal. We've all known that this was coming. That this challenge was inevitable.

Picket 5 (*runs on*) Cortonwood, Manvers, Dykehead, Cornsay, Kinglassie, Shotton: *solid*!

Cheering, and now a police presence.

Picket 6 Seven weeks, lads, and we'll have won.

Picket 5 If our union had not accepted this challenge it would've rolled over and died in shame.

Picket 6 Well, alright then, ten weeks max.

Picket 1 There's blokes out with us. Blokes in good pits. In safe pits. On good money. With families. But they're out.

Picket 3 It's our pit they wanna shut today but it could be yours tomorrow.

Picket 7 (*runs on*) Sharlston, Beamish, Billerly Crags, Annesley, Brayton Domain: *solid*!

Cheering. Now even more police . . .

Picket 7 Stand with us! Stand with us!

Picket 4 What do you want to do – stick yer heed in sand? You don't need a ballot to tell you what's right and wrong and this strike is *right*.

Picket 2 If we lose this strike, if we sell out our jobs, can our sons buy it back? No, 'cause there'll be nowt left. From pits to dole.

Picket 1 Blairhall, Scotswood, Pentwyn, Edge Green, Tulligarth, Shirebrook: *solid*!

Picket 3 There's a downside to mining and we all know it.

Picket 5 Everything we have, somewhere down line, somebody's had to put up a fight for it.

Picket 6 Our fathers.

Picket 2 Our grandfathers.

Picket 4 Our great-grandfathers.

Picket 1 Have had to stand their ground.

Picket 2 Have fought.

Picket 3 Have starved.

Picket 4 None of 'em wanted to do it.

Picket 6 It's our turn now, lads.

Picket 5 Our struggle today is not about what we stand to gain.

Picket 4 It's aboot what we stand to lose.

The mass of pickets now move forward as one heaving body, one booming voice.

Pickets Brucefield. Risehow. Golborne. Warsop Main. Babbington. Walkmill. Argyll. Tankersley. May Green. Monckton . . .

A picket wearing a Thatcher mask breaks from the mass body.

Thatcher (*to us*) I must tell you that what we have got here is an attempt to substitute the rule of the mob for the rule of the law. And *it must not succeed*! *It must not* SUCCEED!

Scene splits: picket and police clashes, and MacGregor's office.

MacGregor Eleven pits, Peter. In four days I have eleven pits open and they're not even cutting coal. The men are playing poker down there! You have got to put a stop to the mass picketing. In the US the National Guard would have been brought in by now.

Walker Yes, well, this isn't America.

MacGregor You have the legislation to stop picketing at *any* premises that are *not* the pickets' own.

Walker If we enforce that piece of anti-trade union legislation now –

MacGregor Which we have the right to do –

Walker It will bring out the other unions, it will bring out the TUC, and then frankly we're fucked.

MacGregor It will stop the mass picketing and get men back to work.

Walker The answer is not legislation, the answer is more police.

MacGregor We already have police.

Walker Not on the scale we're about to deploy. And not with the powers. You have to trust me on this. I know most of the Cabinet sees not enforcing the Employment Act as compromise, as the actions of a wet. But then most of the Cabinet thinks the coalfields are on Mars. We already have seamen refusing to touch coal. Dockers refusing. Railmen refusing and that's *without* their union's say-so.

MacGregor So fire 'em!

Walker Their unions have threatened to strike if members are sacked for supporting the miners.

MacGregor Who the hell runs this damn country?!

Walker Yes, we have posed that question before. If we enforce the Employment Act it will bring out the *entire* labour movement in protest. The miners must be left isolated. (*Pause.*) There's one more thing. Something I really need to discuss with you – David Hart.

MacGregor I spoke to David on the phone yesterday.

Walker You know he's supposed to be running the 'Back to Work' campaign?

MacGregor Sure, we talked about that.

Walker You know he lives in *Claridge's*?

MacGregor He gave me the number of his hotel suite.

Walker And you know that running a miners' strike from Claridge's is frankly ludicrous?

MacGregor He's been putting the miles in, he's already visited half the coalfields of the Midlands.

Walker I need you with me on this.

MacGregor You know I worked with his brother at Lehman's? (*Chuckles.*) It's a small world.

Walker The Prime Minister is . . . is taken with him and cannot see –

MacGregor I like him too.

Walker He's an avant-garde film-maker, for Christ's sake!

MacGregor I thought property was his thing?

Walker It was. Then he lost it, spent it, and went bankrupt.

MacGregor Well that sure shows something, a man who can bounce back.

Walker With a spectacular inheritance, yes.

MacGregor Look, Peter, I admit . . . he's irregular.

Walker He wears jodhpurs!

MacGregor Jodhpurs?

Walker Riding trousers when he's not riding, pilot helmets when he's not flying, and tennis shoes with *pin-striped suits*! If I didn't know he kept mistresses up and down the country, I'd say he was a poof. And that's who we're sending to the *miners*? To encourage them back to work when he hasn't done a day of it? Surely you can see it's not going to work. How are they going to relate to him?

MacGregor Well, when we spoke on the phone, he told me about his schooldays at Eton.

Peter wants to laugh but can't . . .

Hold on a minute. I don't know if you know this but . . . he's a Jew. He had a rough old time there at Eton. Anti-Semitic stuff. Nasty. Really vicious bullying. His experiences confirmed to me that there will be many men out there wanting to stand up to the bully boys, and David's the man to help them do it. He's a deeply ideological person, a libertarian, and has experience in political activism.

Walker (*scoffs*) Such as?

MacGregor He's what I'd call a professional anti-communist.

Walker The 'Back to Work' campaign is the linchpin to the strike. We have got to get it right.

MacGregor And you gotta trust *me* on this. David's going to be reporting for *The Times* newspaper as a feature writer on the strike. His focus will be Nottinghamshire, telling the stories of aggrieved men and women. In the course of time David will encourage and assist these people to form a union of their own: a union of *democratic* mineworkers. And he's putting the money up for it.

Walker (*changes his tune*) He is?

MacGregor nods and smiles. Walker makes to leave.

MacGregor So, Peter, are we gonna keep those pussycat police in Nottinghamshire or are we gonna get in some real red-blooded western sheriffs?

Walker Westerns: we're sending in the *Met*.

THE OCCUPATION

An army of riot police march on stage . . . The shields part, a large desk is revealed.

The shields configure into walls: Tilsley's office. A cocky, brusque Chief of the Met.

Tilsley Welcome to Nottinghamshire. Have you been to these parts before?

Chief Can't say I have. No need to really. I've heard of it.

Tilsley Sherwood Forest. Robin Hood.

Chief Five women to every man. That true?

Tilsley Not in this village, no. I was told on the phone there would be a Metropolitan Police unit here at the pit?

Chief That's right, and four hundred in the village, more if there's trouble.

Tilsley Four hundred? This is a tiny village. Where are you all staying?

Chief Army barracks, Leicestershire. Hotels aren't an option given how many men I've got. And your men, how many have you got working?

Tilsley We aren't cutting coal.

Chief How many?

Tilsley Five. (*Beat.*) But given what happened at Ollerton.

Chief The dead picket?

Tilsley David Jones. I hear it was a brick that killed him, thrown by a miner going to work.

Chief There's a lot of talk flying about.

Tilsley Before that he'd been badly beaten.

Chief Far's I'm aware no one saw what happened.

Tilsley I heard it was by a police officer.

Chief Pickets are bound to say that, of course, but a proper investigation will say otherwise.

Tilsley The place looks like a war zone – upturned cars, boarded-up windows.

Chief You been over there, have you?

Tilsley To see the manager of the pit.

Chief Friend of yours? Sympathetic to the strike, I hear. Advising men to stay at home.

Tilsley Where did you hear that?

Chief I don't always believe what I hear, something you learn in this job: there's always people with an axe to grind. But there have been reports. Men not feeling supported who want to work. Which is why we're here. To make sure they are, supported. To make sure this village sees that. And that this pit starts cutting coal. (*Stands.*) Where's my office?

The shields reconfigure, moving rapidly like a shoal of fish. The desk disappears.
 Pithead in the distance, the police have now formed a line. They shout to pickets . . .

– Shut it scum!

– Get back to work, you lazy bastard!

– I said fucking shut it!

– Come 'ere and wet this truncheon.

– Oy you, move!

Colonel, Bobbo, Fanny, Jimmy, pickets and police: the atmosphere bubbles . . .

Colonel Shutting pits when they're prepared to pay for them lousy bleeders.

Jimmy Forking out £350,000 a day for 'em. That's just here, Nottinghamshire. On radio that.

Fanny Our Lorraine got fright of her life this morning when she opened front door.

Jimmy Me mam too. She dropped pint a' milk on doorstep, woke us all up.

Bobbo I've never seen nothing like this. This is something else.

Helicopter passes overhead, dogs bark and resist their chains.

Jimmy Way I see it: government's holding all aces but we can kick table over.

Colonel Well, that is one fucking great bastard plan.

Bobbo The plan is picketing. Twenty-four seven. Three shifts.

Jimmy Shifts? I might as well as be back down pit.

Colonel Welcome to the picket line. Eight-hour shifts.

Fanny Four in a morning starts.

Colonel In bollock-freezing conditions.

Fanny (*gestures police*) New friends.

Bobbo Scabbing old friends.

Colonel And a flask of Baxter's soup.

Fanny Your life for the next . . .?

Colonel Seven weeks.

Jimmy (*hollers*) Hey-up!

Malcom Been looking for yers, could hardly get through. Big turn out, int it?

Jimmy Time to see who's who. Thought you said you weren't coming?

Malcom I had to get out house. Our Janice is driving me crackers.

Colonel She still not happy?

Malcom She's doing my head in. One minute she's off on one, next minute she's crying.

Fanny Why don't you say for her to go to women's group they've set up – Women of Welbeck.

Bobbo I don't reckon much to it, I don't.

Jimmy Why, what's up with it?

Bobbo Should be Ladies of Welbeck.

Colonel Women sounds common.

Fanny That's what I said to our Lorraine.

Bobbo We're miners, we've got standards, so when they're out representing us –

Fanny She said they're representing *themselves*.

Bobbo We'll be having gay pride here next.

Colonel Have a heart-to-heart with her tonight. You know, put your arm around her.

Malcom I did. She drove her elbow into my rib and called me a selfish prick.

Bobbo I remember a time when men were men and women were bloody glad of 'em.

The pickets become vocal.

Jimmy Scab bus must be coming.

Colonel I don't reckon anyone will be on it.

Jimmy Don't be surprised if Spud is. You spoken to him?

Fanny (*quietly*) I don't know what he'll do.

Bobbo Hark at who's driving the bloody thing: Big Ed.

Colonel You're joking? I stood with him in '72.

Bobbo And '74, and we won a bloody settlement!

Malcom (*aside to Jimmy*) It'll be right, won't it?

Jimmy How do you mean?

Malcom We'll win, won't we?

Jimmy Course we will. Seventy-four!

Malcom Seventy-four.

*Jimmy, Malcom, Bobbo have moved to the crowd.
Fanny remains with Colonel.*

Fanny You remember Wally Westwood and Benny Stock?

Colonel Course I do, ah.

Fanny Worked every job together. No matter what it were.

Colonel Inseparable.

Fanny Worked every day of their lives together for . . .?

Colonel Twenty-odd year.

Fanny Then Wally had to pack up early with ill health.

Colonel That's right, lungs.

Fanny Benny couldn't work without him so he packed up two weeks later.

Colonel Way it is for some blokes, one can't be without the other.

Fanny That's me and Spud. I went round his house last night and told him that.

*The police are beating on their shields with their
truncheons. Some shields now break away from the*

line and form a bus, a scab bus . . . Stones are lobbed at it, the three men inside are now visible, one has his coat over his head, Spud stares defiantly ahead. The whole crowd is a furious sea of motion but for Fanny, who stands still. The two of them locked in a stare . . .

Fanny Judas. Judas. JUDAS!

OPERATION ENDURANCE

MacGregor's office.
David Hart wears a sheepskin flying jacket, a pilot's hat with goggles, and smokes with a long cigarette holder. Among friends he's called, most affectionately, Stalin.

MacGregor I want to say how much I appreciate all you've done so far with the 'Back to Work' campaign. But I need to say that this strike is a gloves-off job. I imagine you're a man with commitments of your own but I'd need you to see it through.

David All rehearsals are off, Chairman. The show will *not* go on.

MacGregor Show?

David *The Little Rabbi.* It's a play, one of my own.

MacGregor Play?

David First draft only. But a private performance was pencilled in for next month.

MacGregor I was told you were a film-maker?

David I'm a playwright now, Chairman. I'm a writer who has been thrust into politics. I've known my whole life that I'm a writer – I'm absolutely fascinated by other people – but history develops, Chairman, art stands still. The muse will be there, but history won't wait and these . . . *these are historic times*. Besides, what could I say having had a direct call from the very front?

MacGregor You've been speaking to Peter Walker?

David (*sniffy*) Peter? No, Chairman . . . *the lady*. She actually said to me, as we strolled arm in arm, the fate of this government is in your – and the Chairman's – hands. (*Intoxicated again.*) I love it when she uses her chest tones.

MacGregor On the phone you said about a plan . . . a legal assault against the union?

David I call it the Gulliver Plan. Each legal action brought by working miners against their union will tie a small legal rope. Eventually the union will be tied down by so many writs they will wake up one day unable to move. You see, the union cannot defend itself legally without a ballot.

MacGregor I've a whole list of legal actions we could take, damages to Coal Board property –

David All the legal actions must come from working miners. If you take industrial action you make it political. What we want is *personal*: the assault and intimidation of ordinary men who want to go to work and are being prevented from doing so by hard-left hooligans. We make it personal, it becomes criminal. There's a law for that.

MacGregor I see what you're saying, but where are the miners willing to take their union to court?

David Under the rough coat of the farmer there are very often to be found the instincts of the squire. When in the Midlands I have my ear to the ground and the help of MI5. One can only hope they prove better at counter-subversion than they ever were at unmasking Soviet agents.

MacGregor Then there's the cost of legal actions.

David I know a number of people who are dying to help us with the struggle.

MacGregor I think the idea has potential, but legal wheels turn slowly, it could take months.

David Have you not been told what the code name for the strike is over at the Department of Economic Warfare? Endurance, Chairman. *Operation Endurance.*

MacGregor Time is on our side.

David With power stations able to run off oil if needed, the Electricity Board has privately guaranteed the Prime Minister *indefinite endurance.*

MacGregor However long the strike goes on, the lights won't go out.

David Exactly. Now, I really must leave you, my helicopter is waiting.

THE GULLIVER PLAN

A pub. A few tables are occupied.
    Spud is sitting at the bar, the barman is pulling pints. In walks David Hart. Everyone turns, everyone stares, everyone gets back to their pint. David also sits at the bar, close to Spud. He eyes the newspaper between them.

David Excuse me, may I?

Spud Yeah, it's not mine.

David (*reads*) Nottingham Forest missed the League again. Or are you a rugger man?

Spud Do I know you?

David Terribly sorry. David Hart.

Spud You're not from round here, are you?

David How did you know? (*Bursts out laughing.*)

Everyone turns, everyone stares, shakes their head and sups their pint.

I'm here on business. I'm a freelance journalist.

Spud I'm not interested in talking, thanks.

David I'm not interested in listening. I've spent the whole week listening to countless stories of misery. All I'm interested in now is booze.

Spud Pint of Mansfield's then.

David (*to barman*) Make that two. And two gins, please. I'm assuming ice and lemon is out of the question?

The barman nods: that is correct.

You're a miner?

Spud How you know that?

David Your reaction to me being a journalist. Which colliery?

Spud Welbeck. It's about eight mile away.

David And yet you're drinking here?

Spud I am now, yeah.

David Well, bottoms up. I didn't catch your name.

Spud Spud.

David *Spud?*

Spud It's a nickname. I've a brown birthmark on back of me head in shape of a spud.

David How extraordinary.

Spud Not really, I've had it all me life. It was only when I was a kid you could see it.

David Children can be so cruel.

Spud Me mam called it me first. How long you been up here then?

David A week. I'm supposed to leave tomorrow. But I've decided to stay.

Spud Why? Right now I'd rather be anywhere than round here.

David Yesterday I was in a village called Shirebrook – you must know it?

Spud Not far from here.

David I'd been directed to this house there. When I knocked on the door a woman opened and invited me in for a cup of tea. I noticed as she was pouring the water into the kettle that her hand was shaking. She was terrified. I told her to sit down and that I would make the tea, and once her story came out it was understandable why. Her husband was working, her son was on strike. The family was torn apart. Her house had been vandalised with yellow paint, bricks had been thrown in through all her windows, and in the middle of the night, whilst her husband was at work, her front door had been kicked in. The woman actually seemed on the verge of a nervous breakdown. Her husband had been doing the shopping because she was too afraid to leave the house. It made me so furious, I said to myself, right, I'm going to get involved in this. I'm going to sort these bastards out.

Spud You not catch who's done it.

David I already know who's done it. Arthur Scargill.

That's who's responsible for all of this. This is the way he intends to win his war. Through terror and intimidation. My family are Russian Jews, Spud, I understand what intimidation is. To be marked out as different. We all know how that ends. And these last weeks, I have detected in the air the unmistakable stench of fascism.

Spud Fascism? No, I don't think that. Fanaticism maybe. Yeah, some of 'em are fanatics.

David Arthur Scargill must not be allowed to get his way by terror and intimidation.

Spud I'm not intimidated.

David You're a very brave man.

Spud I don't look at it like that.

David But the rest of us do.

Spud I look at it that *I am right*. The union has denied me my right to vote and have now *ordered* us not to cross picket lines. That we now face disciplinary action if we do?!

David Which raises the question . . . is that legal?

STATE OF SIEGE

MacGregor's office.

David Fifty-six attacks upon homes, ninety-five cars damaged, sixty cases of physical assault and one blinded cat! These are the people – and pets – paying the price for British democracy. These people need us, and they fucking need pit managers!

MacGregor We're working our way through what I'd call our soft spots.

David *Soft?* I've seen mice with bigger bollocks.

MacGregor We've had some problems, a number of them aren't behind the Board.

David Behind you, Chairman, they are defying *you*.

MacGregor I've asked men to step forward if they feel their manager supports the strike.

David I need names. I need scalps. Fucking careers!

MacGregor I got a call personally from a concerned Deputy Manager in Derbyshire. He reported to me that his Manager is in total sympathy with the miners.

David There's mutiny in the ranks because there's weakness from the top! Heads must roll. Pit by pit, street by street, house by house. We roll back the strike from the edges. (*Pulls out a large map.*) Nottinghamshire is where we win the war. I want pit managers knocking on every striker's door. Starting with men who have mortgages, young families . . .

Walker appears. He is quiet and pale. MacGregor and David don't appear to notice.

MacGregor Peter, you know David.

David Peter is one of the few from the Cabinet yet to visit my pile in Suffolk.

MacGregor David's told me about it, sounds like a real artists' retreat.

David My lawns are covered with thespians.

Walker A policewoman has been shot dead outside the Libyan Embassy at St James's Square.

MacGregor and David immediately turn their attention from each other to Walker.

Walker There was a small demo, a machine gun was fired . . .

David A machine gun?

Walker Ten protestors were injured but the policewoman, Yvonne Fletcher, is dead.

MacGregor Who opened fire?

Walker We believe the shots came from within the Libyan Embassy.

David From *within*?

Walker We're preparing for the possibility of more shooting.

David What?

MacGregor You think there could be?

Walker I honestly don't know. The area is being evacuated, marksmen are surrounding the building. (*Beat.*) I hardly need to say how damaging this could be for us.

David looks from Walker to MacGregor.

David Damaging how?

MacGregor Libya supplies us oil.

Walker It's too early to tell how, *if* it will affect our relationship.

MacGregor We're nowhere near the point of needing oil. We have coal stocks.

David If oil became a problem we could import foreign coal.

Walker Not from the French, the Polish, bloody Australians. They're in league with the union.

David Everyone has their price.

Walker The dockers would refuse to touch it. It would bring them out in protest.

David So what do you suggest?

Walker That I speak to the Foreign Office and see the situation doesn't escalate further.

News

The Libyan leader, Colonel Gaddafi, has responded to the surrounding of the Libyan embassy in St James's Square with a siege of the British Embassy in Tripoli. Eighteen British diplomats are now being held hostage . . . SAS special projects team have been deployed . . . Intense negotiations are under way . . . The eleven-day siege has come to an end, all diplomatic ties with Libya have now been severed.

STICKS AND STONES

The men are picketing, Bobbo and Colonel are sitting on two odd kitchen chairs.

Colonel I got in car and went to Co-op. I couldn't have been inside more than ten minutes. I comes back to car and sees a scratch all down one side on it. Then I see a sticker on me window, a small sticker, and it says You Have Just Met The Met.

Bobbo The bastards.

Colonel Remember them riots in Brixton? I remember watching it happen on telly. Police getting stuck in, giving Pakis and coloureds a proper hammering. And I can remember it now, me thinking, well they'll have been up to no good. Police don't just go off like that – smashing lads up for nowt. (*Half laughs.*) I don't know, some

80

days . . . it's like I don't know where I am. I've come up from underground and I don't recognise what I see.

Fanny Where were you picketing yesterday?

Jimmy Coking plant.

Bobbo (*interjects*) I don't bloody know why. We've got our hands full at pitheads.

Colonel This last week feels like we're wasting our breath.

Fanny I'm not just here to change their minds. I'm here to shame them.

Jimmy Good luck with that. Most on 'em's brazen. Actually proud of scabbing.

Bobbo They believe our pits are safe, don't they?

Jimmy That's why I like going guerrilla, feels like you're doing somert.

Bobbo Going *guerrilla*?

Jimmy Guerrilla picketing, youth. Need-to-know basis. But we're targeting coking plants.

Bobbo If there were no scabs in Nottinghamshire there wouldn't be no scab coal for plants.

Jimmy There won't be power cuts if we don't get to plants.

Malcom (*frustrated*) There's not gonna be any power cuts! They've got mountains of coal.

Fanny It's all lies. Misinformation.

Malcom That's not what he said.

Jimmy (*beat*) Who said?

Malcom Tilsley.

Bobbo (*sharp*) When you been talking to Tilsley?

Malcom He came round ours last night.

Bobbo He did what?

Malcom I dint let him in. Our Janice did.

Bobbo Since when's this been?

Jimmy First I've heard of it.

Colonel He knows better than to come knocking on my door.

Fanny And mine. (*Pointedly.*) So why's he go to yours?

Malcom I don't know. (*Beat.*) What yous looking like that for?

Colonel What's he say?

Malcom Enough coal for six months. That there were two hundred back in pit.

Jimmy Are there fuck.

Malcom And why weren't I.

Bobbo I hope you told him why.

Malcom I'm here, aren't I?

Another awkward quiet.

Jimmy Anyway, it was pretty boring picketing coking plant. Took ages getting there, plus the usual arguments about which route to take. We finally gets there, middle of nowhere it was. We stood in road. Lorries with coal turned back. And that were that. Nowt happened.

Bobbo That's the whole point.

Jimmy Not a copper in sight.

Bobbo How many times – the coppers are an *obstacle* to the target, not *the* target.

Jimmy That's what I'm saying, there was no obstacle. So after a while me and some youths went for a quencher.

Bobbo You did what?!

Jimmy Found a nice pub, sat outside, and set world to rights with a pint.

Bobbo You're there to stop scab coal, not top up your bloody tans and have a piss up!

Jimmy Helps keep spirit up though, don't it?

Bobbo It's not bloody spirits that's going to win this strike. It's strategy and discipline.

Jimmy I'm doing my duty.

Bobbo I'm reporting you to committee and having you barred from picketing.

Jimmy You should come along.

Fanny I don't fancy getting me head kicked in, thanks.

Jimmy You get a quid for it.

Bobbo You're giving that pound back too.

Jimmy And one of these babies.

Bobbo What the bleedin' hell . . .?

Jimmy A Black Widow catapult.

Fanny Cool.

Colonel What you been up to with that?

Jimmy Nowt. Self-defence. And I took out a rabbit for me dinner.

Malcom Can I get one?

Jimmy We got given a whole box of 'em from these London anarchists.

Bobbo London anarchists?! This strike's unpopular-e-fucking-nough.

Colonel It don't look good on telly, that don't. Turns folk against us.

Fanny Nowt looks good from our side on telly, youth.

Jimmy Me mam said she saw me on telly.

Fanny Case in fucking point.

They laugh but for Malcom.

Malcom How are we gonna make do on eleven pound a week? (*Beat.*) How we gonna do it?

Jimmy A pint's one pound ten.

Malcom I'm talking about providing for my family, Jimmy.

Fanny Our Lorraine and me mam are organising a buy-an-extra-tin appeal tomorrow.

Malcom Soup kitchens and food parcels don't pay bills.

Bobbo Speak to committee about an hardship payment, the women's been raising money.

Malcom I have. It's three pound per family.

Colonel The union should be giving lads strike pay, that's what we pay union subs for.

Jimmy That painting and decorating job not come through, then?

Malcom No. The bloke's brother got laid off so he took him instead.

Jimmy Fair enough.

Malcom Yeah but it don't help me, does it?

Jimmy It's a few more week of hardship, youth.

Malcom Few more week . . . ?

Colonel It's gonna be longer than that.

Fanny It can't be more than a few month.

Malcom Few month . . . ?

Bobbo However long it takes –

Malcom Me and Janice have got ten days! We've got ten days. To pay what we owe. Or they're coming for furniture.

Fanny Lorraine's got a meeting with bank next week, ask if they'll freeze our mortgage.

Bobbo Your Janice still not behind strike?

Malcom I tried talking to her yesterday. Tried to have a nice day, just me and her. We borrowed car to take us to seaside. Thought we'd go for a walk, have an ice cream. We got stopped at a checkpoint in Mansfield and told to turn back or be arrested. 'We suspect you are pickets. We suspect you will cause a breach of peace.' She's not said a word to me since.

Two Police approach.

Police 1 Keep it up, lads, I'm going on a Caribbean holiday with the overtime.

Police 2 Your King Arthur's paying off our mortgages.

Police 1 (*waves twenty-quid notes*) Time and a half. (*Laughs.*) Time-and-a-fucking-half.

Suddenly Malcom grabs a stone and lobs it at Police 1, who staggers down.

Police 2 Are you alright?

Chief arrives on the scene.

Chief Don't any of you bastards move! Which one of you bastards was it?

Bobbo I'm here.

Chief (*to Police 2*) Nick him.

Malcom No!

Jimmy Don't hit him.

Chief Nick 'em all!

A brawl. Jimmy and Bobbo are swallowed in the swell of heaving bodies. Pickets and police shouting and pushing. The Colonel pulls Malcom out from the swell.

Colonel Stay here.

Malcom I've got to –

Colonel No!

Malcom I've got –

Colonel Stay here or you'll be arrested as well.

Jimmy and Bobbo are dragged away. Pickets and police action breaking up.

Malcom I can't do it no more. I can't . . . I killed . . . killed dog. I couldn't feed her. Can't even feed a fucking dog. Took her up woods. Was gonna leave her there. Honest I was. But daft sod kept following me. Had her since she was a pup. Told Janice she ran out in front of a car. She'd never forgive me. Dint know what else to do.

A restaurant in the Midlands.

David So how have you been?

Spud Alright. You?

David *Dreadful.* I feel like Birmingham.

Spud I want to thank you for seeing me tonight.

David The pleasure's mine. How did you find our meeting last week?

Spud Yeah, it was alright.

David I felt it was important for you all to meet, to see that you aren't alone.

Spud There were more blokes there than I thought there'd be.

David And what men you are. The backbone of this country, Darren.

Spud I dint really speak to most of 'em. Everybody was pretty quiet.

David Everyone's waiting. Waiting for the man who will make the first move.

Spud I want to talk to you about it. You know. Just go over it again.

David Everything will be taken care of, the case, the solicitor, the fees.

Spud And I'd be issuing writs against the union.

David You'd be arguing that the strike in Nottinghamshire is not official.

Spud Which it's not.

David The court will judge the strike unofficial and you will have won.

Spud What will I have won?

David Your right to work.

Spud But I'm already at work.

David You will deal the union a huge financial blow, the start of many.

Spud But it's not going to change the minds of them on strike.

David There are many men on strike, Darren, that do not want to be. Four of the men at last week's meeting are on strike. Too scared of what will happen to their wives, their children, their pets and their homes if they go to work. Scared of being branded a scab. There are many decent, hard-working people out there who just want to get on with it. And you. You will be an inspiration to them all. There'll be interviews.

Spud Interviews?

David People will want to know who this lion is. What makes him tick?

Spud You're saying I should see this as an opportunity?

David Your name will be known up and down the country.

Spud If I go ahead and do this it'll change everything for me. Permanently.

David I can guarantee you twenty-four-hour protection, former SAS –

Spud What? You've got be joking. I'd have to move. I'd have to do something else.

David And let Arthur's thugs win?

Spud I wouldn't mind doing somert else. That's what I've been thinking. I wouldn't mind.

David Whatever you want, Darren, whatever *you* want.

Spud I started down pit when I was sixteen. Loved it straight away, couldn't wait to get down. I'd grown up on pitman stories from me father – the camaraderie, the crack, and the craft. When I was nineteen I got to drive the cutter, that's the machine that cuts the coal, for first time. It's a big thing that. A really big thing to drive the cutter, only older blokes do it. But down pit if you're hard-working and respectful you get given a chance. Anyway, I did a good job of it, and I was excited, you know? For first time in me life I felt like I'd really achieved somert. And when I got home and told me father, he was like, 'You dint, did you?!' And I was like, 'I did! I did!' He was dead proud, you know. Dead proud. (*Beat.*) When my father was dying, two year ago now, he asked to be cremated. Me mam was upset about that. She dint want to go and talk to a gravestone. She wanted him down there. So one day, when we're alone together, I talk to him about it. I say, what's it matter, you're dead anyway, if it gives me mam some comfort. And he raises himself off his pillow, points his finger at me, and says, 'I've spent most of my life down there and when I'm dead *I am not going back down.*' (*Beat.*) And I was . . . so fucking angry. I felt . . . cheated. Like I'd been sold muck for diamonds. What I'd been made to believe all these years was precious was dust. The pit . . . it's just what we've got. What we've made it be for us. When I think about it now, it don't make me angry, it makes me sad. Me father wasn't deceiving me, he was deceiving himself. So when you say to me, if that's what I want. I don't know what I want. I've never asked myself that question. I don't think people round here do.

David Seems to me you are in need of inspiration. A trip to London perhaps?

Spud To London?

David (*raises his glass*) To new horizons.

Spud New horizons.

NEGOTIATIONS

MacGregor's office. Now looking dishevelled, he could be living there.

David Every newspaper. Every newspaper that matters: *Times*, *Sun*, *Mail*, *Mirror* has the photo front page. (*Beat.*) What were you doing with a plastic bag over your head?

MacGregor It was a joke.

David Go on.

MacGregor I'm having this secret meeting with Scargill that the press aren't supposed to know about. So when I got out of the car I thought, I know, I'll put a plastic bag over my head: can't you see I'm not here? (*Chuckles.*) You know my sense of humour.

David Deliciously eccentric but over the heads of many. Over the heads of the miners, Chairman. *Way over* their heads. To them this photo says, I'm scared of Arthur Scargill. And if I'm scared of Arthur Scargill you should be too.

MacGregor I think the value of PR is overstated. I don't see why it's necessary for me to be involved at all, especially when they print this stuff after all our cosy meetings.

David Think of it this way, as there's no government involvement in the strike and I'm just a journalist for *The Times*, who will take all the credit for bringing the miners to heel? *Sir* Ian – (*Winks.*) That's who. Now what was said at the meeting with Scargill?

MacGregor I let him know what I'm thinking about the pits – Cortonwood, Polmaise, Snowdown –

David What are you thinking?

MacGregor I reckon I'll be able to use them as a trade. You see, Scargill's tacked a great deal of importance to those pits.

David What do you mean, 'trade'?

MacGregor In the scheme of things they don't matter much to me.

David You're suggesting a trade with Yorkshire's answer to Stalin?

MacGregor Two are close to the end their coal reserves, Cortonwood was never meant to close –

David There can be *no trade*.

MacGregor I'll be coming away with what I want in return.

David What you want is *everything*.

MacGregor David, in tough labour negotiations like these –

David These are *not* negotiations!

MacGregor I am gonna have to give an inch to take my yard.

David *Anything* you hand that red prick he will parade as victory. Is that what you want, to humiliate her? Then you give him nothing. (*Beat.*) You know Chairman, there were no returns to work this week, not a single man, because of the hope such meetings bring.

MacGregor Peter says I have to have these meetings.

David Peter Walker is a wet, a weak-willed, embittered failure of the Conservative Party.

MacGregor He says it's politically expedient.

David Our strategy is not negotiations, it's getting fifty-one per cent back to work. We get fifty-one per cent back and it's over, the strike collapses.

MacGregor But we don't have anywhere near those numbers.

David But we will, Chairman.

MacGregor I'm not producing coal, I'm losing my export contracts, I'm –

David (*breathes deeply*) Operation Endurance . . .

MacGregor (*breathes deeply*) Operation Endurance. Time is on our side.

David Now for the fun part of the day. (*Reads a newspaper.*) 'There has been a massive haemorrhage of talent from the mining communities. It is the diluted human residues that remain, especially in Yorkshire and Durham. Five years in the E-stream of comprehensive schools . . . (*Sniggers.*) is an excellent training in sheer bloody-mindedness.' (*Smiles.*) *Human residues.*

   Walker appears.

MacGregor Ah, Peter, David and I were having a quick catch-up on events.

David (*smugly to Walker*) Easily done, now I have an office here. In three months I've covered thirty-five thousand miles and have eaten in every miserable restaurant the Midlands has to offer. When I saw Claridge's this morning I wept . . .

Walker hands a report to MacGregor. He just stares as MacGregor reads . . .

But I now have twenty-five cells, seventy-five working miners. One of them a very promising Nottinghamshire man willing to go to court. (*Looks.*) What is it?

MacGregor (*reads*) There's six weeks of coal stocks at the power stations.

David What?

MacGregor After that the amount of oil needed before running into difficulty –

Walker Difficulty?!

MacGregor – is 350,000 tonnes of oil imports a week.

Walker That's a *sixfold increase*!

David Will it keep the lights on?

Walker That's twenty million pounds a week. Twenty million a week. Every single week.

David And the lights stay on?

Walker Yes. If we had it. But we don't.

David Where do we . . . ? Oh. (*Beat.*) The mad dog.

Walker How much coal can you deliver?

MacGregor (*incredulous*) *Deliver?* Peter I . . . ?

Walker At the pitheads in Nottinghamshire, some of them are now producing?

MacGregor There's not more than a million tonnes.

David How do we know Gaddafi won't deliver?

Walker We're not exactly friends at the moment.

David He stands to gain twenty million a week.

Walker Or he might just settle for the downfall of this government instead.

MacGregor We're not able to move any of the coal stocks from the Nottinghamshire pitheads.

Walker We know. Norman wants to open a second front. Take on the rail workers.

David And give Scargill a wet dream?!

Walker I've always insisted that the miners remain isolated but –

David Over my dead fucking body!

Walker The railmen are drastically reducing the transport of coal. We're running out of options.

David And you're handing him the TU-fucking-C.

Walker I have just come from a meeting with Margaret talking about bringing in the troops.

MacGregor I've always said, if this was America . . .

Walker She is this close. She was jotting down figures for how many troops were needed.

David Does she want a General bloody Strike?!

Walker She wants the coal stocks moved from the pitheads. The rail men won't do it.

David What have you employed non-union road hauliers for?

Walker There aren't enough, and the picketing means they don't always get through.

MacGregor So use the Employment Act to stop the flying picketing in Nottinghamshire.

Walker That only helps at the pitheads, their tactic is to target lorries en route, power stations.

David The answer's not the Employment Act. The answer's . . . to give them something.

Walker What are you talking about?

David Something that turns their attention away from Nottinghamshire.

Walker What?

David Something more important. Somewhere else.

Walker There is nothing more important and they know it.

David It's what they *don't know* that matters, what we can make them believe.

Walker (*to himself*) We're staring into the abyss.

David A new battleground. A distraction.

Walker slumps into a chair. After a beat, he holds up the paper on MacGregor's desk.

Walker What were you doing with a plastic bag over your head?

MacGregor It was a joke.

Walker And to top it all it's a Harrods bag. I mean *Harrods?*

CLARIDGE'S

Above: an opulent but on-its-way-to-being-trashed hotel room. Loud music.
All sorts of characters: businessman, bankers, artists. Someone's playing an electric guitar in the corner of the room. Spud walks in looking like something out of

Scarface, *cigar in one hand, bottle of champagne in the other. He takes his place in the middle of the couch. David Hart squeals with delight as the cocaine comes out: the credit cards chop it, the banknotes snort it.*

Guest (*shouts to Spud*) All done with *money*!

Below: the last of the furniture is being removed, blankets and a duvet are thrown on the floor as a bed is removed by heavies. Malcom sits on the floor. A baby cries. He brings a letter out from his pocket and reads. MacGregor appears dreamily to Malcom, Tilsley also appears with his letter. Their dialogue overlaps.

MacGregor Dear Colleague . . . you have already seen your savings disappear . . . strike until December . . . many years for you to recover financially . . . more jobs will be lost . . . if we have a lengthy strike many pits are in danger of never reopening . . .

Tilsley There has been a return to work . . . you are now in the minority . . . the last hundred men to return may not find employment . . . I need to know your position in planning the future manning of the colliery . . .

ROAD TO ORGREAVE

A major road. Early morning.
The men are merrily singing a strike protest/solidarity song. The car slows.

Jimmy I said there'd be roadblocks, what did I say?

Malcom We're not gonna get through.

Bobbo We should be in own backyards anyway. All pickets should be.

Colonel (*to Fanny*) Get map out.

Bobbo Not fannying about at Orgreave.

Jimmy You not be saying that when we've clinched strike.

Bobbo Shutting down one coking plant not clinch nowt, shutting Nottingham pits will.

Jimmy Yeah, well, Arthur's told us shutting Orgreave is essential.

Bobbo Napoleon said invading Russia was.

Colonel (*to Fanny*) See what radio says for roadblocks.

Bobbo There's no surprise. The coppers know we're coming.

Jimmy It just needs one final push to shut it.

Bobbo Lads have been there every day for last two weeks. We should be in Nottingham.

Jimmy I fucking you wish you were.

Colonel (*with the map*) I can't make head or tail of this, I don't know where I am.

Jimmy (*to Colonel*) Here give it me.

Malcom In '72 Arthur shut Saltley coking plant and it clinched strike.

Bobbo 'Arthur shut'? You mean thousands of workers down-tooled and joined miners.

Jimmy And they're going to again.

Bobbo And while you're dreaming, coal production's going up in our pits.

Fanny (*to himself*) Spud?

Bobbo As we stake everything on a bloody field!

Fanny (*turning the radio up*) Shurrup, it's Spud!

Radio Unprecedented action of issuing writs against the National Union of Mineworkers at both the area and national level . . . (*Static cuts in.*)

Fanny It's Spud. Darren Winters. She said Darren Winters.

Malcom What's issuing writs?

Bobbo Taking union to court.

Malcom What for?

Jimmy Check another broadcast.

Colonel It can't be him.

Fanny Darren Winters.

Colonel It can't be.

Fanny She said Darren Winters.

Bobbo Whoever it is –

Jimmy Fucking over his own union.

Colonel No. He's fucking us.

Fanny I feel sick.

Two Policemen are approaching.

Jimmy Here we go. Company.

Police 1 Where are you going?

Bobbo Fishing.

Police 1 Out the car. All of you.

They pile out the car.

Driver's licence. Keys.

Colonel hands it over. Police 2 opens the boot with them. Police 1 and the Colonel stand opposite each other. Police 1 just stares at the Colonel. Police 2 checks through the fishing tackle. Up ahead a fight appears to be breaking out. A Policeman is showing an Officer weapons: catapults and so on, The two Pickets are being led away. One of them shouts.

Picket 1 One of ours is dead! Another one of ours is DEAD!

The men look at each other, shocked. The Colonel looks into the eyes of Police 1 who just continues to stare at him; they remain like that. Picket 2 shouts before being wrestled off:

Picket 2 (*handcuffs raised*) This is England!

Police 2 comes back from the boot, shakes his head: nothing.

Bobbo (*choked but with brio*) Well. Can we bloody well go now?

Jimmy looks terrified at Bobbo's lip. Police 1 hands the licence back to Colonel.

Police 1 Turn around and fuck off back.

Police 2 You heard him.

Police 1 Two minutes before you're all nicked.

They all move back to the car but for the Colonel.

Deaf as well as thick. I said fuck off.

Colonel This is England.

Police 1 Fucking. Move.

Colonel This is England.

Police 1 MOVE.

Colonel This is England.

Police 1 And you're nicked.

Officer appears.

Officer What's going on?

Police 1 Obstructing me in the course of my duty, sir.

Officer If he's not carrying anything let him go.

Colonel is freed. Police 1 looks at his superior.

(*Smiles.*) Let them go to Orgreave.

ORGREAVE

Above: David Hart, the Chief and Special Branch, with binoculars.

Chief It's a good site.

David It's perfect.

Chief A battleground of our choosing.

David How many pickets are we expecting?

Chief Biggest turn-out yet, eight to ten thousand.

David We want lots of arrests. Criminal fucking records.

Chief All the pickets are to be rounded up into this field. We'll have fifty Ops amongst them.

Below, the scene is set: an Operative dressed in jeans and short-sleeved shirt runs on.

Operative (*hollers*) Come on then, pass it.

He receives the football, kicks it off, watches it fly, speaks into shirt collar . . .

Target B is wearing a flat cap and is bare-chested. Eagle tattoo on his right arm.

Operative cheers, runs off. Head Set sets up her position.

Head Set All units, Carrier One is heading on to Parkway. That's three minutes for Carrier One.

Chief The first lorry is due to arrive at ten thirty. We've got surveillance in the air.

Pilot (*voice only*) Carrier One is in sight. Now heading off Parkway Road.

Chief Inside the disused chemical factory is where the command post is. On the perimeter of the field we want police and dogs to both the east and west sides. To the north mounted cavalry, foot soldiers, shields ten deep. Their only way out is to the south across the railway lines.

David And the wood?

Chief If they make it through, a thousand police will be waiting on the other side.

Special Branch We'll have regiments in reserve. (*Smiles.*) Northern Ireland all over again.

David (*laughs*) Updated for Yorkshire.

Chief What about the media?

David They won't be in uniform and journalists will be behind police lines.

Chief The BBC will be here.

David Not to worry, their footage will show miners attacking first.

Head Set All units, Carrier One is in two minutes.

David When William the Conqueror invaded England, the strongest resistance, most bitter warfare he encountered, was in the North. Once defeated, those villages were punished with both famine and sword, in what became known as the Devastation of the North.

Such was the devastation that many, many years later those places were still worth nothing. Orgreave was known as Or*grave*.

Head Set All units, Carrier One is in one minute.

David Their hopes of victory will be buried here. At Or*grave*.

Below: medieval war drums pound out their battle cry. They climax.

A sword-swinging Saxon warrior runs out, stakes his sword into the ground.

He cries out to us in Old English: 'Olicrosee!' His soldiers reply: 'Ut! Ut! Ut!'

Picket (*with a tannoy*) Maggieee!

Miners Out! Out! Out!

And the battle begins. The sound of chinking armour. Riot police march on stage.

Head Set All units, Carrier One is imminent.

Pickets Here we go.

Chief Hold the line!

Pickets Here we go.

Chief Hold it!

Pickets Here we go.

Chief Hold!

Pickets *Push!*

The shields react: sound of a massive heave, medieval-like scrum, almighty roar.

Scab! Scab! Scab! Scab! Scab!

Pilot (*voice-only*) Carrier One has passed into the plant. Pickets are now in retreat.

Head Set All units, pickets are in retreat. Stand by.

Operative Target B is heading south.

Chief Close ranks!

The shields close, truncheons beat on them.

Operative Target D is on the move.

Head Set All Field Ops prepare: horses are imminent.

Pilot (*voice-only*) I repeat pickets are in *retreat*.

Chief Cavalry!

The shields part, out canter horses: panicked Pickets are heard to cry out.

Close ranks!

The shields close. The shields retreat backwards.

Short shields!

The shields part, out run short-shield and truncheon-bearing squads:

– Down you go!

– Shut your fucking mouth!

Chief Bodies not heads!

– Fucking Yorkie miner!

– Break your fucking neck!

Chief I said bodies NOT HEADS!

Out of the choreographed chaos, a new situation emerges:

Operative I have a new target: yellow T-shirt between two transits on Parkway Road.

Head Set Copy that. Target's status?

Operative Target has footage of soldier in military uniform in transit van.

Special Branch MPs in pursuit *now*.

Head Set All MPs, priority target: yellow T-shirt in possession of camera, Parkway Road.

Operative Yellow T-shirt is now heading off Parkway.

Special Branch Where the fuck are our MPs?

MP Coming off Parkway now.

Chief Oy! Nick that bastard, he's got a camera!

Operative Yellow T-shirt being pursued by police.

Special Branch Fuck's sake. There'll lose him!

MP Target in sight, on the run.

Operative Yellow T-shirt heading for the crowds.

Special Branch We cannot afford to lose this bastard!

Operative That's it. Police have got him.

Special Branch Get the camera.

Head Set MPs to retrieve the camera from the police.

Operative Yellow T-shirt does not have the camera.

Special Branch Fuck.

Operative Camera's in the crowd.

Special Branch Fuck it.

Operative Camera is lost.

The choreography changes, another situation emerges:

Chief (*into walkie-talkie*) Which fucking idiot knocked down Arthur Scragill? Over.

Police (*into walkie-talkie*) Don't know. Over.

Chief (*into walkie-talkie*) Well fucking find out! Over.

Police (*into walkie-talkie*) He's unconscious. Over.

Chief (*into walkie-talkie*) He'll fucking love that!

Head Set All MPs in pursuit.

Operative 1 Target B heading for the railway tracks – That's it, he's down. He's down. He's nicked.

Head Set I repeat all MPs, Unit One in pursuit.

Pilot (*voice-over*) Police are now entering residential area.

Police 1 Asda car park, we've got a situation here, request medic immediately.

MP (*out of breath*) I've lost him. Residents are opening up their houses.

Operative 1 Oh shit. Shit! He's gone purple! His head's gone *fucking purple*!

Special Branch Storm the houses.

Head Set (*looks for a beat at Special Branch*) Permission to pursue.

Pilot (*voice-over*) I repeat, police are now running charges into RESIDENTIAL AREA.

> *Police 1 is performing the kiss of life on a Picket.*
> *Police 2 is freaking out.*
> *Scenes from a battlefield: despair, confusion, anger, violence, chaos.*
> *And then, an almighty explosion. Windows shatter. Bricks collapse. Fires burn.*
> *Everyone reacts to the explosion; bodies convulse. Peter Walker appears.*

Walker (*to us*) Brighton. I'm supposed to be here. The Prime Minister and the Cabinet are all here at the Grand in Brighton for the Party conference. But the pressures of the strike convince me to stay in London. Sir Anthony Berry takes my place. At 2:54 a.m. a bomb explodes. He is killed instantly. Eric Taylor, Lady Jeanne Shattock, Lady Muriel Maclean and Roberta Wakeham all die from the blast. Thirty-four people are taken to hospital. Margaret Tebbit is paralysed from the neck down. Arthur Scargill . . . has saved my life. The Prime Minister insists the conference goes ahead, that she deliver her speech as planned. A remarkable act of personal courage. One she will not waste.

Thatcher It seems that there are some who are out to destroy any properly elected government. They are out to bring down the framework of law. This is what we have seen in this strike . . . (*Clapping.*) Let me make it absolutely clear the miners' strike was not of this government's seeking nor of its making. They did not want a settlement; they wanted a strike. (*Clapping.*) The nation faces what is probably the most testing crisis of our time, the battle between the extremists and the rest . . . (*Clapping.*) This Government *will not* weaken. This nation *will meet* that challenge. *Democracy will prevail.*

End of Act Two. No interval.

Act Three

SPOIL TIP

Fanny, Malcom, Jimmy, Bobbo and the Colonel dig and
sieve for coal in the bitter cold.
    They have a production line of a sort going. Jimmy is
on a break with the newspaper.

Bobbo That's a piece of coal that.

Fanny Where?

Bobbo That bit you've chucked out.

Fanny It's no more than dust.

Bobbo It'll burn, youth. It'll burn.

Jimmy Says here IRA planted bomb *three weeks* before
Maggie's conference.

Colonel And still the daft bastards missed.

Fanny Surprised it don't say we did it.

Bobbo I'm surprised we bloody dint.

Jimmy Rest on, it's just having a go at us over Libya.

Colonel Is that what you call it, 'having a go'? The
papers are having a field day.

Bobbo It's not going to go away, that's not.

Jimmy There were some good Gaddafi jokes going round
on picket last night.

Colonel I'm not laughing, youth.

Fanny It was pretty fucking stupid.

Malcom But papers' reactions right over top.

Colonel Over top? Our union went cap in hand to Libya to a bloody terrorist for money!

Bobbo If it helps lads stay out longer it can come from Satan, never mind Gaddafi.

Fanny (*firmly*) It's lost us support.

Jimmy Has it hell? I'm past caring what shit they print about us.

Fanny My Lorraine was in street yesterday fundraising and right in her face got told to fuck off back to Libya. So don't tell me –

Malcom They were there to tell Gaddafi to stop supplying Maggie oil.

Colonel They were there for money!

Bobbo They were doing both.

Jimmy *Mail* reckons it were guns.

Malcom There's no mention of oil in papers though, is there? No mention of what all that extra oil's costing. Don't talk to me about cost. Not when she's spending sixty-five million quid a week on strike.

Jimmy Sixty-five million. Every fucking week.

Bobbo Never spent a round coin here before.

Fanny Let's see what she spends after.

Bobbo Come on then, you, Fanny's on a break now.

Jimmy I've not had me twenty minutes yet.

Bobbo Above ground it's ten.

Fanny and Jimmy exchange places.

Fanny Few week and it's Christmas. Our Jason wants a Transformer. Three pound fifty. (*Beat.*) I came home last night from picket – been out since four in morning, freezing it was, lagging it down, police hammering every one of us, we runs away, police runs after us, we runs back to cars, police smashes every one of our window screens – and I stood there on top of our landing looking out window into next door's kitchen. All sat round table they were. Roast chicken they'd got. A full roast chicken. Stuffing. Taters. Vegetables. Like a Bisto advert. I wanted the scabbing bastard to choke on it. Him. His wife. And his fat fucking kids.

Beat.

Colonel Food parcels are coming in today.

Malcom Me and Janice got a Swedish one last week.

Jimmy Quite exciting int it, when it's foreign?

Malcom There was a lot of funny stuff in it. Janice says we're getting to taste all foods of world.

Bobbo That's one way of looking at it.

Jimmy You should have heard his Janice at Saturday's rally.

Fanny She was speaking, was she?

Malcom After Tony Benn. Imagine? No way could I of done that.

Jimmy Crowd went mental for her.

Malcom She got a standing ovation. Thought you were coming?

Fanny Our Jason's not very well, he's been poorly for last couple of week.

Colonel What do you reckon to my Saturday afternoon? There I am, minding my own business with a crossword, when there's a knock on door. So I opens it, before I know where I am the bloke's in me house with this sack and a Hoover. Turns out he's a Hoover salesman. Anyway, he walks straight into lounge, and without saying a word about it to me, chucks a sack of soil on me carpet. A full sack of soil. Then he takes this here Hoover and says to me, don't worry, performs miracles it does. I said it better fucking do, I've had no electricity for twelve week.

They laugh, long and hard. Security Guard, Daniel Hargreaves, appears.

Security What's going on here?

Bobbo We're digging for coal.

Security I can see that.

Fanny Hey-up. Hey-up, it's Craig. Craig Fannshore.

Security I don't know you.

Fanny We were in same class at school.

Security Look, I don't know you, but –

Fanny Daniel! Daniel Hargreaves.

Security I'm the security guard for these premises.

Colonel Security?

Security Yeah, so what you doing with that?

Bobbo We're taking it home.

Security It's National Coal Board property.

Colonel You what?

Bobbo We've been digging bloody hours for this.

Security Don't matter. I still can't let you nick it.

Bobbo Nick it?! We're miners, how do you think it got up here in bloody first place?

Security Yeah, well, if it's coal you want get back to work.

Jimmy (*to Fanny*) You say this bloke's a mate of yours?

Malcom Come on, youth, I mean what's it to you if we take it?

Security It's my job, is what.

Jimmy Some fucking job.

Security Well at least I don't expect taxpayer to keep me in one, unlike you lazy bastards.

Tilsley What's going on here?!

Colonel and Security break apart. Only now does Tilsley see it's Colonel and vice versa. Tilsley awkwardly turns away and observes the operation – sieves, sacks, etc.

Security I've told 'em its Coal Board property they're stealing.

The men all turn and look at Tilsley, who finally turns to Security.

Tilsley (*to Security*) They're to empty the sacks.

Tilsley leaves. Colonel's sack spills on the ground as if it were his guts.

Fanny Daniel? Daniel, please.

Bobbo (*stern*) Leave it be, Fanny.

Fanny I know you're doing your job.

Bobbo We'll not fucking beg, I say!

Fanny I really need this coal.

Security And I really need this job.

Fanny I've got two kids.

Security So have I.

Fanny One of 'em's ill, please. (*Offers a handful of coal.*) Look, I'll give you half. I'll give you –

Security (*scatters it*) I don't want half! (*Embarrassed, angry.*) Now empty the fucking bag!

Fanny empties it. Security cops sight of someone else with coal and pursues.

Security Oy you, get back here!

Jimmy We should take it anyway.

Malcom He'll do us for theft.

Jimmy Don't see as it matters.

Malcom We'll lose our jobs.

Fanny Jobs? What fucking jobs? Are we miners? Are we six feet tall? Are we *men*?!

He walks off. Malcom makes to go after him . . .

Bobbo Leave him. I'll speak to him.

The Colonel has been sitting down on the dirt. He looks out, almost absently.

Colonel I've worked seven days a week most of my life. Six, seven, sometimes eight weeks pass before having a rest day. My choice. I've worked like that to provide. And I've taken great pride in providing. When I've packed up and retired, I'll walk down street, sit in Club, and people will nod their heads – young men, old men – and say to themselves: ah, I know him, he's seen some graft, he was a real worker. And I don't think you can ask for any more than that out of life really. To be remembered as a worker. To be respected for it. I don't ask for any more than that. I've never asked for any more.

MacGregor's office: MacGregor hunched over his desk, popping aspirins, Walker and Hart standing either side of him.

MacGregor It's a perfectly viable settlement.

David It's monstrous!

Walker There's phrases like 'pits being deemed exhausted' without saying *who* deems it!

MacGregor I am the Chairman of the National Coal Board.

David And you kept it from us.

MacGregor I've been working on it.

Walker You've undermined the Prime Minister's position.

MacGregor I don't know how much longer I can take this.

Walker Not a single concession, those are her words.

MacGregor I'm an old man, my blood pressure.

David The time for talks is over.

MacGregor But you said I had to keep negotiating.

Walker I said you need to *appear* to be negotiating. Not actually doing it.

David You've won, Chairman. It doesn't matter now how long it plays out now.

Walker now puts his briefcase down.

Walker I've been told that you two paid a visit to John Paul Getty.

David The dear man's frightfully ill.

Walker He's in hospital. And you and Rasputin here sat at his bedside with open chequebooks.

MacGregor What was our thinking there, David?

David He was extremely confused, he'd made a donation to the striking miners' fund.

MacGregor Another one of their children died over the weekend, Peter.

Walker (*awkward*) Yes, I know.

MacGregor A little girl out picking for coal, crushed or buried or something.

David He wanted to help, I told him the best way to do that was by donating to the working miners' fund.

Walker You do not tell a man like that where he can and can't put his money. He is one of our biggest campaign donors. Do not bother him again.

David I see the press are still picking over the Gaddafi affair. (*Reads.*) 'A Nation's Revulsion. Energy Secretary, Peter Walker, said Mr Scargill's support is slipping away as members become disgusted with a political strike which relies on Libyan paymasters.' Bravo, Peter.

Walker Yes, well, we've got some bad press of our own now to deal with. (*Hands paper to MacGregor.*) The Bishop of Durham has publicly attacked the government over the strike.

MacGregor (*to David*) Is he a communist?

David He's a Christian.

Walker He used his enthronement ceremony to do it. He's called for your dismissal.

David Which isn't very Christian.

Walker The Prime Minister is furious.

David It distresses her when people don't see her policies as the purest distillation of Christianity. The parable of the talents being a direct call from Christ for an entrepreneurial society.

Walker We think we need a spokesman. Someone who can . . . appeal to the press.

David Why bother?

Walker Because it's not over yet.

David It's finished.

Walker We don't have half of the men back at work yet.

David We have indefinite endurance, the union haemorrhaging money in court.

Walker Some of us aren't arrogant enough to assume we will survive our own victory.

MacGregor What do you suggest, Peter?

Walker We've got to show we care. Someone who can reflect that we do obviously care.

David Christmas is around the corner: women shaking their begging buckets in the snow.

Walker looks at David with genuine revulsion.

I'm saying, you're right. It will be a tricky time for us.

Walker Let me be clear, I take no pleasure in their suffering.

MacGregor Hell, none of us do. It's just a by-product of trying to do business with a Marxist.

Walker I'll let you know when I appoint the new spokesman.

David But it will be you who will take us to the finishing line.

MacGregor Total victory. Nothing less.

David And you, *Sir* Ian, will be feted as Wellington after Waterloo. They're finished.

MacGregor Even Scargill must know it.

David He knows it.

MacGregor Everybody knows it.

David and MacGregor chuckle.

Walker (*quietly*) Everybody except the men and women of the coalfields.

News
There are frightening scenes in Yorkshire as the return to work has now begun. More than 850 police officers were injured, the number of injured pickets is unknown . . . Strikers bought down power lines while building barricades . . . Arthur Scargill has denied today's Coal Board figures saying three-quarters of his members are still on strike.

THOU SHALT NOT CROSS

The pithead looming down. The sun coming up.
Malcom, Bobbo and Jimmy around a brazier.

Jimmy So the pickets had been told there could only be six of them outside Silverwood pit. So what do they do? They went and built a seventh out of a snowman. Next morning, Chief Inspector Nesbitt appears on the scene and orders the constables to knock it down. At which point a rebellion in the ranks breaks out because they refused to do it. Said they weren't going to look so fucking stupid knocking down a snowman picket. Very well, shouts Nesbitt, who does no more than jump into his Range Rover and at full speed charges into snowman.

Meanwhile the pickets are pissing themselves, because what Nesbitt don't know, is that they've built the snowman around a concrete fucking bollard. Total fucking write-off.

They laugh. Colonel appears.

What time do you call this, shirker?

Malcom Got your foot stuck in your missus's nighty?

Colonel I've got a head as bad as a bastard.

Malcom Where's your coin to go out on piss?

Bobbo Aye, where were you?

Colonel Where do you think? Home. It's not gonna be at Club no more is it, with all scabs.

Malcom Chuck's gone back. Went back last night. (*Beat.*) You're not surprised?

Colonel It's all these rumours flying about.

Bobbo Ah, well, that's all they are, rumours.

Jimmy You mean men that's been out for a year will be sacked?

Colonel It's the medical, getting my back up. Enforced medicals on men out for a year.

Bobbo It's just scabs putting it about.

Colonel No way I'd pass it with dust on my lungs. (*Beat.*) Any new faces this morning?

Jimmy No. They're not gonna now though, with union conference all week.

Bobbo Nowt'll get decided this week. Too much up in air still.

Fanny appears.

Bobbo Hey-up?

Malcom Thought you were down London?

Jimmy No work? I told you that. Endo's got a right gob on him.

Colonel Thousands of us down there now.

Bobbo Should've stayed put. We need all men with cars we can get.

Jimmy Not got car, sold it.

Colonel I bet you got a song for it. Garages, furniture shops, been making a killing out of us.

Jimmy It was on its last legs. All bonnet bashed. Ready for scrap heap.

Bobbo I know how it feels.

Fanny I'm going back. To work.

Jimmy shakes his head bitterly at Fanny and walks off, joins the other pickets.

Bobbo You've got be out your bloody mind.

Malcom You can't go back *now*.

Colonel The union's in meetings this week.

Malcom It's gonna end soon.

Fanny I can't see no end.

Malcom We can still win if we –

Fanny I can't do it no more. I'm done.

Bobbo Then I've nothing more to say to you.

Bobbo walks off and joins Jimmy. Malcom stands apart, letting Colonel speak.

Colonel You've been out for eleven month.

Fanny I can't do another day.

Colonel Eleven month, son!

Fanny fights back his tears.

This isn't you. Not you.

Fanny You don't know me.

Colonel I bloody well do.

Fanny I dint go to London for work. I went to beg. To fucking beg.

Colonel You stupid sod!

Fanny Not for me. For kids.

Colonel You should've come to me. To me.

Fanny No pride. Nothing.

Colonel Not nothing. Not a scab. That's worth more than anything. I knew your father, and he would have been stood here today. Shoulder to shoulder. No matter what had befallen him. Because you don't break the commandment, son. Thou shalt not cross a picket line. Thou shalt not undermine another working man. Not when all he's fighting for is his livelihood. His whole way of life. That's just been written off by some cunt's pen. (*Pause.*) You've been out. But no matter when it ends, if you go back, you won't have been solid. (*Beat.*) You'll be a scab.

Fanny (*wipes his face*) I know.

Colonel nods and steps aside. Fanny looks at the pithead. And walks.

Malcom We can't just let him walk in. (*Beat.*) We can't let him scab now.

Colonel says nothing. Fanny is through the gates.

Malcom Scab!

Colonel (*furious*) He's not a pit idiot! He's a good man.

Malcom *We're all good men!* We're all good men. But not when we –

Pickets cheer. Malcom and Colonel turn and see the Pickets embracing, Jimmy with his head in his hands crouched on the floor and Bobbo frozen still.

Malcom What's going on?

Colonel says nothing, he turns away from Malcom, who now goes to Jimmy.

What's up? (*Beat.*) Jimmy?!

Jimmy Ninety-eight to ninety-one for a return.

Malcom What? What you on about?

Picket 1 Been decided, ant it?

Malcom I don't understand.

Picket 2 Starting back Monday.

Malcom You what? How . . . how's that?

Jimmy How can it just end like that?

Malcom It's not ended!

Picket 1 and Picket 2 walk off, shaking their heads.

So after everything we've been through, we walk back with nothing?

Picket 1 (*calls back*) It's not with nothing.

Malcom Don't give me the 'struggle is the victory' bullshit.

Jimmy A year . . . just like that.

Malcom It's not ended!

Colonel It's over, kid. It's over.

No one says anything as this sinks in.

Malcom What about all men that have been sacked? We're out until there's amnesty. There are men sacked just for striking. Loyal, good men, who have given everything. Watched their wives and kiddies go without. Stood on picket lines in all weathers. Been beaten up by police and spoken to like dogs. Proud working men treated like dogs. Their tears, their blood, their families, their hopes. And now we walk back to work without 'em?! We're out until she gives them amnesty.

Bobbo She won't. She won't give us anything.

Malcom I HATE HER! I hate her. (*He cries.*) I hate her.

LONG KNIVES

David Hart in his silk dressing gown, brandy in one hand, phone in the other.

David The Chairman please . . . David bloody Hart, that's who! . . . I need to speak to him now . . . I need . . . You're not listening to me – governments listen to me, so why the fuck aren't you? . . . Number Ten?

He slams the phone down. He reels, he sweats, he dials.

David Hart here . . . Well, thank you . . . Unavailable? . . . I'll tell her myself, thank you . . . In fact, yes. Tell her without me this strike would have been lost.

He puts the receiver down. Then he slams it down. And again. He sulks. Spud appears wearing a tail coat and hat.

(*Sharp.*) What is it?!

Spud Car's out front.

David There's been a change of plan. I don't feel well. I'm staying here.

Spud Oh. Okay.

David (*all charm again*) How are you settling in?

Spud Not bad, yeah. Different, you know?

David It's not too late to take up my offer.

Spud David.

David Darren Winters, President of the Union of Democratic Mineworkers.

Spud I told you, I don't want to be a union man. Time for somert else.

David I hear they're marching back with their banners and brass bands. A pathetic gesture.

Spud I won't be there to see it. Like I say, I've moved on.

David You and me both. It struck me today that I have this pile in Suffolk and what I really want to do is be a farmer. Build up a shoot there. And a lake.

He makes to pour a glass of brandy but the bottle is empty.

Be a pal and fetch me another bottle of brandy.

Spud Yeah, course.

David Oh, and Darren, you're doing awfully well but how about addressing me a little more formally?

Spud (*beat*) Yes, sir.

David (*smiles*) Perfect.

Tilsley's office: Tilsley stands smoking a cigar, big as a baby's arm.

Tilsley Take your cap off then, lad.

Malcom Why? I've come for a bollocking not a haircut.

Pause. Malcom takes off his flat cap.

I want to come back to pit, Gaffer.

Tilsley Very well. (*Beat.*) That's all. This industry's fucked. I'm retiring.

Malcom Retiring?

Tilsley My successor will be here within the month. He'll be younger, of course. This new breed of managers are. Dynamic, open to suggestion, different style altogether really, which is to say he'll walk into the pit and you won't know who the fuck he is.

Malcom Well, like you say, coal's fucked.

Tilsley They've broken King Arthur. They haven't broken King Coal. The only way they can do that is by making coal a minor player. That means changing the government's entire energy policy. Eighty per cent of our electricity comes from domestic coal. But a rigging of the market in favour of the vastly more subsidised and expensive nuclear industry and gas can change that. But even then we will still need coal to make up for where those industries fall short, so we'll import it from somewhere else. Where men work in the conditions your fathers worked in, where deaths are a normal occurrence, and wages a pittance. Meanwhile, the most advanced mining industry in the world, billions of pounds of investment, and one of our most skilled workforces will be sacrificed and laid at the altar of a new god and all, *all* that is *solid* . . . (*Pause.*) You can go.

Malcom All that is solid melts into air, all that holy is profaned, and man is at last compelled to face with sober senses, his real conditions of his life, and relations with his kind . . . Marx, Mr Tilsley.

He leaves. Tilsley once more picks up his paperwork, but tosses it aside.

THE COST OF AN IDEA

Underground: coaling face.
At the end of the face the Colonel is talking to another miner; they are referring to the scaffolding before them. The previous shift are putting their gear back on when Jimmy, Malcom, Fanny and Bobbo walk on to the face. Everyone looks, glares, nods or ignores.

Jimmy Looks like a cavity.

Malcom Welcome back, eh.

Jimmy I don't know if I can do it, Malc.

Malcom What you mean?

Jimmy I've been dreading it.

Malcom Like riding on a bike. Just got get back on.

Fanny is standing alone when Miner 1 approaches.

Miner 1 Alright?

Fanny Not bad. You?

Miner 1 I've had better shifts.

Fanny What we got then?

Miner 1 About twenty foot high, dint want to leave it for you.

He looks at Bobbo and turns back to Fanny. Before leaving he says:

Watch your back, eh.

Jimmy and Malc join Bobbo.

Jimmy What's he say about cavity?

Bobbo Don't know, couldn't hear.

Jimmy Who shall we ask?

Bobbo No one. They're all scabs.

The Colonel is approaching with Harris.

Malcom You're fucking joking.

Jimmy What?

Malcom Not him, not fucking him.

Colonel You all know Harris. He's our new driver.

No one, Fanny included, says anything.

Harris Don't worry, I feel same.

Bobbo I doubt that.

Colonel That's enough! (*Beat.*) You three on materials now.

Harris, Malcom and Jimmy leave.

You two with me.

Bobbo and Fanny look at each other and look away. They walk to the cavity in silence.

It's not that high, about ten foot.

Bobbo Looks loose to me.

Colonel Why I want to have a proper look.

Fanny steps under the cavity.

Fanny, you watch it for us. Fanny?

Vooom! Tonnes of earth and rock collapse. The men cry out, unseen, as thick dust sweeps through the face. And then a deep silence. Colonel and Bobbo emerge. They stare at each other for a moment.

(*Spins round.*) Fanny?!

Fanny cries out in pain.

I'm here, youth. I'm here.

Colonel navigates his way around the fallen load. Fanny is pinned waist down.

Are you alright?

Fanny Just get this bastard off of me. Just get me out.

Colonel I'm gonna call it now.

Fanny You're getting me out, eh?

Colonel I'm getting you out. I'm calling it in. Just hold on.

Colonel moves back over to Bobbo, who is standing motionless in a state of shock.

I'm gonna call it in. You stay here with him. But you're to stand clear of it until we make it safe. Keep talking to him while I'm gone . . . (*Slaps his face.*) If you don't keep talking to him he's going to go into shock. That's your job. Keep talking. Keep reassuring.

Colonel runs off. Bobbo stares out. Fanny cries out in pain. Bobbo stares out.

Fanny Tony? (*Beat.*) Tony?

Bobbo He's not here. (*Beat.*) I am.

Fanny (*pause*) I can't feel me legs.

Bobbo (*beat*) That's alright.

Fanny I can't feel nothing downwards.

Bobbo You probably not be kicking a ball about for a week.

Fanny You'll get me out, eh?

Bobbo Course we will. Men will be on their way now.

Fanny You'll get a lather on shifting this lot.

Bobbo We've eaten through loads like this before.

Bitting spits out from the cavity. Bobbo looks up, uneasy.
A howling wind rushes down the shaft – Colonel shouts into the phone.

Colonel Craig Fannshore . . . Check number 638 . . . He's trapped from a roof fall . . . District Seven . . . Get flying paramedics . . . Let Gaffer know . . . It's bad, Tommy. It's bad.

Above: Tilsley's office.
Tilsley puts the phone down. Tips his head back. This is it. The phone call.

Tilsley Hello, is your mother there . . . ? Could I speak to her please . . . ? It's John Tilsley, Mrs Fannshore . . . Yes, I'm afraid there's been accident . . . No, no, he's trapped . . . Yes, yes, we're getting him out . . . Do you need someone to pick you up . . . ? And what about the children, shall I send . . . ? Alright, Mrs Fannshore . . . Yes, we will.

Below: men are swarming about the site, grabbing shovels.

Colonel How you doing?

Fanny Ah, you know.

Colonel We're getting it off. We're gonna move this debris. Get you a bit more comfortable.

Fanny I say, we getting a pint in after, sluice down some of this dust?

Colonel I'm gonna go home, take a shit and go to bed. We need to put up some support.

Jimmy We'll start timbering.

Colonel (*to Bobbo*) You stay talking to him.

Jimmy Can we get him out?

Colonel Course we can.

Jimmy I mean . . . in time?

> *Men start on the shovel, the rhythm of their shovelling marks the pace of a ticking clock.*
> *Time passes . . .*

Bobbo Your Lorraine's here.

Fanny Where is she?

Bobbo On pit top.

Fanny She knows how I am?

Bobbo She knows we're getting you out, yeah.

Fanny Let her know I'm alright.

Bobbo She knows that. She's just here to go to hospital with you.

Fanny You're getting me out, eh?

Bobbo It's coming off now, kid.

Fanny I don't want to her to be worried, youth.

Bobbo She's not. She's come here to give you a good bollocking.

Malcom Perhaps we should slow down?

Fanny Definitely.

They all laugh. Colonel and Tilsley are standing to one side.

Tilsley How long's he been under?

Colonel Thirty-six minutes.

Tilsley (*looks down and away*) Christ.

Colonel No. No. Look at him.

Tilsley His organs have been crushed, poisonous toxins have now entered his bloodstream –

Colonel But look at him, he's laughing, he's talking, he's . . .

Tilsley He's dead, Tony. Dead. Twenty minutes . . .

Colonel I know. That's all the time a trapped man's got. After that you're talking to a ghost.

Time passes . . . Each time we see the men who are recovering Fanny more exhausted.

I'm gonna give him more morphine.

Bobbo More? He's gonna be out of it.

Colonel Just keep him talking.

Bobbo We need to get him up in time. To say cheerio. To his Lorraine. To his lads.

Colonel I know.

Bobbo It's a big thing that. To say cheerio.

Time passes . . . Men are still at it, men are shattered, men are refusing to take breaks.

Fanny Here because of – our grey meadows
our black castles on top of village hills

our pit tips – our grey meadows
thieves on our own lands they call us – thieves
for they are ancient battles these
our army no longer on the march
surrender surrender you are surrounded
our army tired and cold
surrender now and be punished not
our flags raised – on and on – stupid pride
why fight when you cannot win
but they are ancient battles these
so they raid our castles – tear down our flags

The men are now off shovels, scrambling to remove
rocks with their hands.

I'm the son of a son of a son of a collier's son
the last in a long line
for it all ends here my sons
the filling of pits – halting of marches
singing of our songs – music of our bands
forgive them not – for they know what they do
when they take away our life blood
strip us of our pride
leave us on pit tips
covering up our long history
where bloody battles have been fought and won
and won – where work of dignity has been done
with blades of grass – they will erase our past
bury their swords and cover their tracks
so that when they come to our ravaged villages
look around our boarded-up towns
because of the choices you make – they will tell us
because of the choices you make
and then they will leave –
and we will fight amongst ourselves
who has only two children who has four
which have fathers which don't

our bands mute – our hymns forgotten
who has a disability who really don't
our stories – our myths – our giants
low-life – shirker – salt dissolved into scum
our long march halted – our voice –

Fanny's breathing becomes a rapid intake of breath.

Colonel We've got him.

Bobbo He's going into shock!

Tilsley Put him down, down!

Colonel Stand back!

Bobbo He's going, he's going.

Colonel I need space!

*He performs resuscitation on Fanny, his breathing
a distressing intake of sharp breaths. Tilsley puts his
hand on Colonel's shoulder. He eventually stops the
resuscitation. Fanny in a whisper . . .*

Fanny
But hear this
for there will be another march
you are outnumbered
we will be marching with them
a black and avenging army of ghosts
arise arise
sons and daughters

Arise!

*The roofing now begins to give way, bitting and earth
trickling down.*

The state spent £6 billion to win the strike

Three children died picking coal from colliery waste
heaps in winter

Three miners died on picket lines, one man died driving a miner to work

Three miners committed suicide while on strike

Twenty thousand miners were hospitalised, 9,808 were arrested, 1,849 were sacked

The state went on to spend £60 billion dismantling the coal industry

Forty per cent of our energy still comes from coal, most of which is imported

In 1991 the BBC acknowledged that the events of Orgreave had been mistakenly edited

In 1994 three ex-mining communities were classified by the EU as the most deprived areas in Europe

Heroin use is twenty-seven per cent above the national average in ex-mining communities

The men begin to fossilise: reduce down to teeth and bone.

There is a last dying breath from the pit.

Their head lamps flicker and with an almighty explosion are extinguished.

Blackout.